BEYOND THEIR YEARS

BEYOND THEIR YEARS

Stories of Sixteen Civil War Children

SCOTTI COHN

TWODOT®

Guilford, Connecticut
Helena, Montana
An imprint of The Globe Pequot Press

A · TWODOT® · BOOK

Cover photo courtesy of the Library of Congress, LC-USZC4-7983

Library of Congress Cataloging-in-Publication Data
Cohn, Scotti.
   Beyond their years : stories of sixteen Civil War children / Scotti Cohn.
      p. cm.
   Includes bibliographical references.
   ISBN 0-7627-1027-6
   1. United States—History—Civil War, 1861-1865—Participation, Juvenile. 2. United States—History—Civil War, 1861-1865—Children. 3. Children—United States—History—19th century. 4. Teenagers—United States—History—19th century. I. Title.

E540.C47 C64 2002
973.7'0835—dc21   2002072076

Manufactured in the United States of America
First Edition/Second Printing

To Ray
for yesterday, today, and tomorrow

CONTENTS

Acknowledgments   ix
Introduction   xi

Union

The Natural and Accepted Order of Existence
Jesse Root Grant   1

"Sojer Boy, Will You Marry Me?"
Maggie Campbell   11

And Then the Trouble Began
Edwin Fitzgerald (Foy)   20

A Drop of Blood for Every Tear
Ella Sheppard   28

Little Red Cap
Ransom Powell   38

"I Can and Shall Never Forget"
Susie Baker King   47

Bound to Go
Elisha Stockwell Jr.   56

A Straw to Hold
John Henry Crowder   65

Confederate

"I Wanted to Fight to Music"
Opie Percival Read   74

Little Rebel
Rose Greenhow   85

Flashes of Bursting Bombs
Eliza Lord   94

"We Cannot Win"
Anne Augusta Banister   104

Young in the Ghastly Game
John Sergeant Wise   112

The Light in the Window
Sallie LeConte   122

A Perfect Sheet of Bullets
Albert Butler Blocker   132

Want of Leadership
William H. S. Burgwyn   142

Bibliography   152
Index   159
About the Author   164

ACKNOWLEDGMENTS

I am tremendously grateful to Silvana R. Siddali of Illinois State University's history department, who reviewed each chapter and provided valuable insight and suggestions. My deep appreciation also goes to my editor, Charlene Patterson, for her feedback and encouragement. In addition, I thank the following people for their assistance: Byron Abernethy, grandson of Elisha Stockwell Jr.; Paul Begley, South Carolina Department of Archives and History; Hubert Bender, Harrison County Historical Museum, Marshall, Texas; Donaly E. Brice, Texas State University and Archives Commission; Melissa Bush, University of Georgia; Robin Copp, University of South Carolina; Dick Dobbins, Historical Data Systems; Armond Fields, author of *Eddie Foy: A Biography of the Early Popular Stage Comedian*; Peggy Fox, Confederate Research Center, Hillsboro, Texas; Eddie Foy III; Jeff Giambrone, Vicksburg-Warren County Historical Society Museum; Beth Howse, Fisk University Library; Diane B. Jacob, Virginia Military Academy; Max S. Lale, author of "The Boy-Bugler of the Third Texas Cavalry: The A. B. Blocker Narrative"; Lorraine M. Lentach, Palm Beach County Genealogical Society; Carolyn Shaw McMillan, descendant of Emma LeConte Furman; Ashleigh Moody, Historic Petersburg Foundation; Darlene Mott, Sam Houston Regional Library and Research Center; John W. O'Neal II, descendant of Rose O'Neal Greenhow; Lyla Stockwell Ragar, granddaughter of Elisha Stockwell Jr.; Diana Reep, author of *Margaret Deland*; Harold Scott, editor of *The Civil War Memoirs of Little Red Cap*; Andrew Ward, author of *Dark Midnight When I Rise*.

INTRODUCTION

T hey waved at passing troops, ran from cannon fire, and hid in caves and cellars. Some longed to fight; others dreamed of peace as they huddled in the shadows of death. They were the sons and daughters of a nation in agony—the children of the American Civil War.

"Some indeed called it the Civil War and still refer to it as such," Confederate Private William Calvin Smith wrote in 1908, "but if it was a Civil War, God pity a people in whose country an uncivil war was ever waged."

The sixteen children profiled in this book would have understood exactly what he meant. Many went on to play significant roles in healing their battle-scarred country. Eddie Foy and Opie Read gave the gift of laughter to those who had sorrowed too long. Ella Sheppard Moore filled the air with music. Susie Baker King Taylor brought the joy of learning to a land weary of war's harsh lessons.

What inspires us most, however, is the resilience of these children during times that devastated many of their adult contemporaries. They provided cheer in the midst of hardship, love in the midst of hostility, and faith in the midst of despair. In doing so, they displayed courage and wisdom beyond their years.

THE NATURAL AND ACCEPTED ORDER OF EXISTENCE

Jesse Root Grant

1858–1934

~

Late in the evening on December 19, 1862, a Federal officer hurried across the spacious lawn of Walter Place in Holly Springs, Mississippi. Quickly he made his way through the sea of army tents surrounding the mansion and passed between the white columns that rose on either side of the front door. The officer bore urgent news: Confederate troops under General Earl Van Dorn were headed for the town.

Union general Ulysses S. Grant had made Holly Springs a storage center for military supplies and had set up his headquarters in Harvey W. Walter's stately brick home. On December 19, however, General Grant was not in residence. He was in Oxford, Mississippi. There, for many weeks, he had been executing his campaign to capture the city of Vicksburg.

The soldier who rapped on the door at Walter Place knew the general was gone. He also knew that Grant's wife, Julia, and four-year-old son, Jesse, were staying in the mansion. They must be sent to safety, to General Grant's headquarters in Oxford.

The escape from Holly Springs became Jesse Grant's earliest recollection of the Civil War. He later wrote: "I remember . . . the

Jesse Root Grant with his parents, Ulysses S. and Julia Grant, 1865.

confusion of our hurried departure, at night, in a box car. I can see the dim, shadowy interior of that empty box car, with mother sitting quietly upon a chair, while I huddled fearfully upon a hastily improvised bed upon the floor as an engine drew us rapidly away."

Jesse Root Grant was born on February 6, 1858. Named for his grandfather on his father's side, he was the fourth child of Ulysses and

Julia Dent Grant. Ulysses S. Grant, a native of Ohio, was a graduate of West Point who had fought in the Mexican War. His wife had been raised near St. Louis, Missouri, on a Southern-style plantation. The Dents were slaveholders, and Julia owned a few slaves, one of whom accompanied her on her travels during the early years of the Civil War. Grant purchased a slave in 1858 but gave him his freedom after only a year. He refused to keep slaves offered him by his wife's family.

The Grants' son Fred was nearly eight years old when Jesse arrived on the scene. Their second son, Ulysses Jr. (nicknamed Buck because he was born in Ohio, "The Buckeye State"); was almost six. Daughter Nellie was two and a half.

When Jesse was born, the Grants were living in a log cabin on Julia Grant's family farm. Not long after Jesse's first birthday, Ulysses gave up farming and went into the real-estate business in St. Louis with his wife's cousin. In August 1860 the family moved to Galena, Illinois. Grant's father had offered him a position in his leather-goods store, which was managed by Grant's brothers, Orvil and Simpson.

Galena was an important center of river trade in 1860. Its location just a short distance up the Galena River from the Mississippi gave ready access to the rest of northwestern Illinois, Iowa, and Wisconsin. Incorporated in 1826, Galena had become a boomtown, thanks to nearby lead mines.

The Grants settled into a brick home among the hills behind the town's business district. Like most toddlers, little Jesse found ways to get himself in trouble. His mother recalled: "At two years old . . . awakening from his noonday nap one day, he espied a pair of his papa's boots lying near, and with much difficulty inserted each little leg in a boot and started downstairs. The result was dreadful. His neck was not broken, but his four front teeth were broken squarely off, and he lay quivering and fainting in my arms."

Jesse's father spent most days working in the leather store. Occasionally he traveled to Iowa to buy animal hides. On a typical evening he arrived home for a well-earned rest, only to be challenged by a small but brave opponent.

"Mister, do you want to fight?" young Jesse would demand.

"I am a man of peace," Grant unfailingly replied, "but I will not be hectored by a person of your size."

Jesse responded by pounding his father's knees with his little fists. Grant crouched down and grabbed him. The two then rolled about on the floor until Grant cried, "I give up. I give up." Proudly, Jesse stepped back and helped his father rise.

According to Jesse his father always "fell upon a bed or the sofa" after the match and "stretched contentedly there." In time it occurred to the boy that his father might not be doing his best to beat him, but the suspicion never hampered his delight with the game.

"Jesse was an open, jolly child," brother Fred recalled. "He teased and played with my father, and they enjoyed one another very much."

After the children had gone to bed each night, Grant read newspapers or books aloud to his wife as she sewed. In the fall of 1860, the papers were filled with speeches and articles concerning the upcoming presidential election. Democrat Stephen A. Douglas seemed the most likely winner. Most people felt the Republican nominee, Abraham Lincoln, did not stand a chance. Lincoln believed that slavery should be allowed to remain in states where it currently existed but should not extend into new territories, and Southern leaders firmly opposed this view. A Georgia newspaper declared that the South would never submit to "such humiliation and degradation as the inauguration of Abraham Lincoln." Southern states refused to even put Lincoln's name on their ballots.

Unfortunately for the South the Democratic party was divided. Northern Democrats had nominated Stephen A. Douglas; a group of Southern Democrats had nominated John C. Breckinridge. In addition the Constitutional Union party had put forth John Bell as a nominee. This division of loyalties among Lincoln's opponents gave him a greater chance of winning the contest than he would otherwise have had. On November 6, after all the votes had been counted, Abraham Lincoln had been elected president of the United States. On December 20 South Carolina seceded from the union. In January and February of 1861, six more states joined South Carolina, forming the Confederate States of America.

On March 4, 1861, Abraham Lincoln was sworn in. The following month, he called for 75,000 volunteers to help reclaim Fort Sumter, which had been captured by Confederates on April 13. In response four more states immediately joined the Confederacy.

In his memoirs Ulysses S. Grant wrote about the situation in Galena: "There were so many more volunteers than had been called for that the question whom to accept was quite embarrassing to the governor. A law was enacted authorizing . . . ten additional regiments."

The commotion did not have much of an effect on Jesse Grant, age three. He was vaguely aware that his father had a new job: "mustering regiments." Mostly, he noticed that Papa did not come home every evening the way he used to.

In September Grant, who by then had been made a brigadier general, assumed command of the district of Cairo, Illinois. Jesse and his mother visited him there. Over the next four years, Jesse would travel with his mother to Mississippi, Tennessee, and Virginia—wherever Grant was headquartered at the time. They were usually accompanied by Julia Grant's personal slave, an African-American woman born and raised on the Dent plantation.

"The war . . . was the natural and accepted order of existence," Jesse wrote later. "When father left mother for a battlefront, his going aroused no more emotion in me than when he left us each morning for the leather store in Galena."

In the summer of 1862, Julia Grant and the children went to see Grant in Corinth, Mississippi. Union troops had occupied the town since the end of May. To Jesse and his sister, Nellie, the highlight of the visit was making footprints in the freshly raked earth of a walkway that extended around the house.

They had been in Corinth a month when Grant sent them away to St. Louis. Confederate forces were headed his way, intent on reclaiming Corinth. After a number of skirmishes within 20 to 30 miles of the town, the two sides clashed fiercely on October 3 and 4. Union troops were victorious, and Grant suggested moving forward against Vicksburg. He wrote in his memoirs that, at the time, "Vicksburg was the only channel . . . connecting the parts of the Confederacy divided by the Mississippi River. So long as it was held by the enemy, the free navigation of the river was prevented. Hence its importance."

That December in Holly Springs, Jesse and his mother narrowly escaped the enemy by taking a hastily arranged midnight trip to Oxford. In late summer 1863 Jesse had another harrowing experience. Vicksburg had fallen to Federal troops on July 4, and Grant had sent for his wife. She and Jesse, now five years old, traveled by steamboat down the Mississippi River. Recalling the journey, Jesse wrote: "I remember a joyous start, and, next, a confusion of crashing noise, and mother striving to dress me, bewildered and cross, in the darkness . . . Our steamboat had been shelled from the shore."

Later Jesse's father explained that even though Union troops occupied Vicksburg, weapons were still stashed at plantations and farms along the shore. It was not unusual for people to drag out the guns "for a hasty shot at some passing boat."

When Jesse arrived at army headquarters in Vicksburg, he saw something that made him forget all about the shelling of the steamboat: a Shetland pony, saddled and ready to ride.

"Before the carriage stopped," he recalled, "I had scrambled out and was climbing into that saddle. Father had secured the pony, and a soldier had made the diminutive saddle and bridle, for me. Life holds but one thrill such as was mine as I sat in that saddle."

The pony, named Rebbie, became Jesse's constant companion. Not surprisingly, Jesse enjoyed everything about his visit to Vicksburg— inspecting the army with his father, playing with toys carved by the soldiers, and eating molasses candy made over a campfire. Jesse was also able to spend time with his oldest brother, Fred, who had been at his father's side during the Vicksburg campaign. Fred was only thirteen at the time, but to Jesse he was "a hero . . . utterly fearless."

Indeed, Fred was a brave boy. On one occasion a sharpshooter shot him in the leg as he rode his horse over the enemy's works with the troops. A Union officer dashed up and asked how Fred was doing. "I am killed!" Fred replied. Fortunately, this was not the case.

"I remember leaving Vicksburg with regret," Jesse wrote.

In the fall of 1863, the five year old found himself in Nashville,

Tennessee. His father had been placed in charge of a campaign against Chattanooga, one of the South's critical rail centers. In November Grant's forces broke the Confederate hold on that city. By then Jesse had begun to understand what his father's job entailed. When told that the Confederates had been whipped in the battle, he inquired anxiously, "Who whipped?"

"Grant," came the answer.

"Hurrah!" Jesse called out joyfully. "Bully for Grant!"

The next city Jesse and his siblings called home was Burlington, New Jersey, about 25 miles from Philadelphia, Pennsylvania.

"As the General had formed a very high opinion of the morale of Philadelphia," Julia Grant wrote in her memoirs, "he wished me to remain there and send the children to school."

Mrs. Grant had heard excellent reports about Burlington's schools from a friend, and quickly made the necessary arrangements. Although she described the town as "delightful" and the people as "kind and hospitable to us," Jesse had a somewhat different experience. He wrote: "There were many Southern sympathizers in Burlington. . . . We three strange boys, sons of the man fighting at the head of the Union army, received a disconcerting amount of the hostile attention. Fred at once took it upon himself to fight my battles as well as his own, and for a time he was very busy. Fred came to be looked upon as invincible; at any rate, I considered him so."

During the summer of 1864, the Union government constructed a huge supply depot at City Point, Virginia, about 20 miles from the Confederate capital at Richmond. Located on a plateau overlooking the junction of the James and Appomattox Rivers, City Point contained more than 280 buildings housing hospitals and support services. Eight wharves served a vast fleet of ships. A network of more than 22 miles of railroad track connected the wharves to Union lines. A highly efficient communication system allowed contact with Washington as well as all Union forces throughout the country.

Ulysses S. Grant, now General-in-Chief of the Union Army, had ordered the creation of the complex "in the very dooryard of the Confederacy," as Jesse later put it. Backed by City Point, his troops could maintain a continuous assault on Petersburg, Virginia. Grant knew that once Petersburg was captured, Richmond would fall.

By March 1865 seven-year-old Jesse was living with his parents in Grant's City Point cabin. The war had gone on much longer than anyone expected. Petersburg was still under siege. The names of battlegrounds such as Antietam, Fredericksburg, and Gettysburg had already become synonymous with grief and horror. Eager to end the death and destruction, President Abraham Lincoln made several trips to City Point to meet with Grant and other military leaders.

Jesse never forgot his first impression of the war-weary president. "The horse President Lincoln rode walked calmly . . . the President sat stiffly erect, the reins hanging slack from his hands. In a tightly buttoned frock coat, and wearing a high hat, Mr. Lincoln appeared enormously tall, much taller than when standing. And to me . . . the unsmiling, worn, but kindly face, the tall black-coated form . . . gave a feeling of awe that time has not effaced."

On one occasion Jesse found out that the president could also ride a galloping horse with considerable skill. Lincoln's twelve-year-old son, Tad, had joined his father at City Point. The two Lincolns, along with Jesse, General Grant, and a military escort, prepared to ride to nearby Fort Stedman.

Tad Lincoln was not a confident horseman, Jesse later recalled. He "demurred at mounting a small, beautiful horse called Jeff, that had been provided for him."

"I can still hear the pride in father's voice," Jesse continued, "as he said, 'Jesse will ride Jeff.'"

With Tad seated on Jesse's pony, Rebbie, the group departed. Jesse and Tad rode ahead, "Rebbie's diminutive hoofs ringing like the beat of a drummer's double time in his efforts to keep pace with Jeff."

Suddenly, Jeff lunged forward and launched into a full gallop. Jesse's father and the somber, dignified Lincoln spurred their mounts and gave chase. In Jesse's words: "All the pull I could exert but steadied Jeff in his stride, and under my feather weight he was widening the gap between us and our pursuers at every bound. . . . Ahead of me men were shouting and running, and a double line of soldiers and teamsters

Jesse Root Grant with his parents circa 1872.

formed as by magic, converging upon the open gate of a mule corral."

The race was over, but the excitement was only beginning. Grant's party had just dismounted at the fort when shells came screaming over their heads. A Confederate battery had opened fire.

Jesse and Tad were delighted. As Jesse put it, this was "the sort of entertainment we most keenly enjoyed." Far from entertained, Grant and Lincoln hurried their sons into a bombproof shelter, where they huddled, "listening to the distant booming of the guns." Unfortunately, Jesse recalled, they couldn't see anything. The boys begged to be allowed to go outside—or at least stick their heads out. The request was denied.

Union troops captured Petersburg on April 2, 1865, forcing the evacuation of Richmond. On April 9 Confederate General Robert E. Lee surrendered to General Ulysses S. Grant at Appomattox Courthouse, Virginia.

"Vaguely, I understood that a change had taken place, that the war was over," Jesse recorded. "Plainly this thing that had happened had made both father and mother happy. But in our family the final act of the drama was never discussed, either then or later."

Five days after the surrender at Appomattox, on April 14, a pro-Confederate actor named John Wilkes Booth shot and killed President Lincoln at Ford's Theater in Washington. Jesse was saddened by the death of the man with the "worn but kindly face." Only later in life did he realize that he came close to suffering a more personal loss that night. His parents had been invited to accompany the Lincolns to the theater, but they had chosen instead to travel back to Burlington with Jesse to see the rest of their children.

In 1868, when Jesse was nearly eleven years old, his father was elected President of the United States. Jesse attended elementary school in Washington. At age sixteen he enrolled in the engineering school at Cornell University; however, there is no record that he continued past his freshman year. After his father's second term as president ended, nineteen-year-old Jesse accompanied his parents on an extended journey across Europe.

Jesse later attended the Law School of Columbia University for one year. At various times he lived in New York and California. He married Elizabeth Chapman in 1880, and they had two children, Nellie and Chapman. In 1897 Jesse was involved in negotiations with the Mexican government to develop a gambling resort at Tia Juana. In 1908 he ran in the presidential primaries on the Democratic ticket but was not nominated. His marriage to Elizabeth ended in divorce, and in 1918 he married Lillian Burns Wilkins.

Jesse Root Grant died on June 8, 1934. He was buried at the Presidio National Burying Ground in San Francisco.

"SOJER BOY, WILL YOU MARRY ME?"

Maggie Campbell

1857–1945

~

M aggie Campbell scooted closer to her Aunt Bessie as the streetcar rattled through downtown Pittsburgh, Pennsylvania, one chilly December day in 1862. Even though she was only five years old, Maggie was already a seasoned streetcar passenger. She was used to the musty smell of the straw that covered the floor, the scratchy plush seats, and the jingle of the bells on the mule's collar. These things were too familiar to hold her interest for long, but the boy across the aisle was a different matter. The brass buttons on his blue uniform glinted in the sunlight. In the straw between his muddy boots sat a drum. Maggie couldn't take her eyes off him.

The streetcar bounced and bumped along Penn Avenue past the Allegheny Arsenal. For the past eighteen months, the Arsenal had supplied the United States Army with gun carriages, armory, ammunition, and military equipment to use against the Confederate States of America. Every day, the *Pittsburgh Gazette* reported victories won and men lost in "The War."

About three months ago, on September 17, a series of explosions had occurred at the Arsenal. Nearly eighty employees had been killed in the blast, most of them women and children. (Small hands and slender fingers were highly suitable for assembling weapons and equipment.) That same day, Union soldiers had clashed with General

Robert E. Lee's troops at Antietam Creek, near Sharpsburg, Maryland. Pittsburgh had lost dozens of its sons in the battle.

To Maggie, however, "The War" meant lively music and cheering. When she shouted "H'rah! H'rah!" at passing troops, grown-ups called her a "dear little patriotic girl." Gazing at the young man with his drum on the streetcar that December afternoon, Maggie thought of a way to garner even more praise. She leaned forward.

"Sojer boy," she said in a loud, eager voice. "Will you marry me?"

Many years later, at age seventy-eight, Margaret Campbell Deland described the incident in her autobiography, *If This Be I, As I Suppose It Be*. Referring to herself as "Maggie," she wrote:

"I even have a dim memory of faces turned towards Maggie; but what difference did that make? There was for her in the whole car, no one but the little drummer, who stared at her, his mouth falling open with astonishment."

Aunt Bessie, her face red with shame and disapproval, gripped Maggie's shoulder and whispered, "Be quiet!" She pulled the strap above the window and dragged her niece off the streetcar as soon as it stopped.

As a dignified, genteel adult, Margaret felt far removed from her childhood self. She admitted that some of her youthful antics were "served up to me when I was a grown woman by amused elders with embarrassingly good memories." She also declared that most of her own memories were "astonishingly clear." She continued: "They float up to me from the depths of the unremembered . . . in such cheerful and complacent certainty of detail . . . indifferent to my ideas of fitness."

The war did not frighten Maggie—at least not at first. She and her cousin Johnny made a game of it. Acting out the words of a popular song, they pretended to hang Confederate President Jefferson Davis "on a sour apple tree." Sometimes they went behind the henhouse, grabbed the hatchet that lay on the chopping block, and pretended to behead the unfortunate Davis.

"[We] took turns in brandishing this horrid implement," she later recalled, "and then bringing it down *whack!* onto the block, exclaiming 'O-o-o-o! He's dead!'"

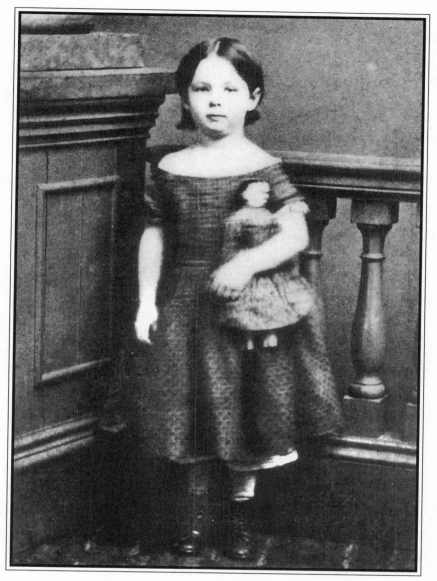

Margaret "Maggie" Campbell circa 1863.

Maggie had no reason to worry about the war. She lived in comfort and safety at Maple Grove, her family's acreage in the Pittsburgh area, above the Ohio River. Maggie's mother, Margaretta Wade Campbell, had died giving birth to Maggie on February 23, 1857. Maggie's father, Sample Campbell, an elderly Kentucky widower, died when his daughter was two weeks old.

Even though she was an orphan, Maggie thrived in what she later called "the large and generous household" of her mother's sister, Lois, and Lois's husband, Benjamin Bakewell Campbell. To her they were "Mama" and "Papa." Their daughter, Nannie, was her "sister." Maggie's sense of belonging was strengthened by the fact that her last name was Campbell, like theirs, even though Sample and Benjamin were not related.

Maggie's life in the western corner of the Keystone State was idyllic. Looking back as an adult, she remembered gazing out "over low-lying meadows, to the gleaming expanse of the Ohio, then far down the river to the rolling mills, and their vast coils of purple-black smoke." The garden was a pleasant spot, bordered by fragrant boxwood shrubs. Maggie would lie on her back under a tree, gazing at the sky "through the flicker of the larch . . . staring up into the blue depth, and watching an occasional cloud moving over it like a white ship!"

The Campbell estate was almost a community in itself. After its first owner died, his children and grandchildren built their houses there. Maggie had countless cousins to play with. One of her favorite activities during the war was watching troop trains puff through the countryside near her home. Accompanied by family and servants, she climbed the grassy bank overlooking the railroad tracks. Everyone tossed fruit, flowers, and candy down to the men. Years later, Margaret described what she saw and heard on those occasions: "Soldiers, sitting on the roofs, their legs hanging over into space; soldiers leaning against each other, or lying full length, with haversacks for pillows; soldiers with bandaged heads, or arms in slings. . . . The soldiers' salutes, their jokes, their bawling snatches of singing—all went to Maggie's head. But wouldn't it go to anybody's head to hear a lot of boys roaring 'The Girl I Left Behind Me'? That's what they sang oftenest."

Some of the women waved their aprons at the troops. The Campbells' gardener, Billy Graham, raised his "broken-brimmed straw hat." Others waved handkerchiefs and "shouted friendly words." Maggie loved being part of the throng. One day, however, her desire to show her support for the soldiers got her in trouble.

Everything was fine at first. It was a lovely, sunny afternoon. As the train came into view, the crowd standing on the bank above the tracks began to cheer. Maggie started to join in, then realized that she had forgotten to bring her handkerchief. She had nothing to wave at the soldiers! Tears began to fill her eyes, but before they could fall, she came up with an idea.

Like most five-year-old girls of her day, Maggie was dressed in layers. Her dress, shorter than an adult's, ended at mid-calf. Under it she wore a knee-length shift called a chemise or "shimmy." Corsets and hoops were reserved for older girls and women, but Maggie did wear petticoats and pantalettes, or "drawers." These extended just below the edge of her dress. Therein lay the solution to her problem—and eventually, the cause of great alarm.

With as much speed as possible, she clambered up the hillside on hands and knees and darted behind a low building that stood near the orchard. A few minutes later, her legs bare, she slipped and slid down the grassy bank, clutching her pantalettes to her chest. In her book Margaret recorded what happened: "Maggie reached the very front of the cheering, flower-flinging group, and, shaking out the drawers, waved them frantically—waved, and screamed, 'H'rah!' Any one who can think back to the incredible 'modesty' of the [18]60s, can imagine the shocked amusement of the aunts, the snickers of the girls."

Mama seized the pantalettes. Maggie was scolded sternly and told she was a dreadful child and that everybody was ashamed of her. She didn't really believe that. For one thing she knew Papa didn't feel that way. When he heard about the incident, he roared with laughter and exclaimed, "Well, at least we have *one* patriot in the family!"

Not long after the pantalette episode, Maggie's schoolmistress, Miss Amanda Wright, married Captain Don Smith, a Union officer. The idea of war took on even more glamour for Maggie at the wedding. Smiling, she watched the handsome soldier kiss his beautiful bride.

It was an especially joyful event for Miss Wright's class, Margaret wrote later. Their teacher—nicknamed "Cousin Pidge" by her students—took a few days off to be with "Captain Don" before he rejoined his regiment. In her place the children were loosely supervised by a young substitute who, as Margaret recalled, "let us do whatever we wanted." Once again, the war had added to Maggie's enjoyment of life. It was a trend that was not to continue.

One morning nearly six weeks after Captain Don departed, Cousin Pidge did not come to school. The children were told that they could go home for the day. Maggie learned that Captain Don had been killed in battle, and she knew her teacher's "sojer boy" would never come home again. When Cousin Pidge finally returned to the classroom, she had changed. Margaret wrote:

"Something had happened to her! She was old. *She didn't laugh*. She didn't even cuddle Maggie, and say 'What! You can read in four letters? Wonderful!' War had turned Cousin Pidge into this silent, frozen creature."

Maggie began to understand that war was not just music and cheering; it caused pain. In the spring of 1863, this view was reinforced. She caught snatches of conversation about "Rebel raiders"—how they killed people, tore up railroad tracks, and stole or destroyed property and possessions. The kitchen servants talked about hiding in the woods. Maggie heard the name "Morgan" whispered in frightened tones, but she could not learn any details. Whenever she entered a room, the grown-ups told each other to "hush."

Pittsburgh's residents had good reason to feel threatened. Their city was close to Pennsylvania's border with West Virginia, where Confederate raids had been reported. In addition, by the end of June, Confederate troops had made their way into south-central Pennsylvania. The entire state was on alert.

In early July Pennsylvania was the setting for the Battle of Gettysburg. On July 4 after three days of fighting, Lee withdrew to Virginia. He had lost seventeen generals and more than one third of his army. The Union seemed stronger than ever, but rumors soon began to spread that Confederate Brigadier General John Hunt Morgan and his band of horsemen were en route to the Keystone State.

Morgan's Raiders were known all too well in the North for their murderous attacks on Union targets in Tennessee and Kentucky. They had invaded Ohio on July 13, producing widespread anxiety in that state.

Maggie hoped "Mr. Morgan," as she thought of him, wouldn't come to Maple Grove and steal her precious chickens. All the whispering and grim expressions worried her, but there was nothing she could do.

One blazing summer afternoon, she decided to go for a walk with her favorite dog, Major. Years later, she wrote: "The wandering took her towards [gardener] Billy Graham's domain. . . . She saw right ahead of her, *half of Billy!* Billy, from his hips up. But as she stared, he bent over and threw out a shovelful of earth, so she knew that his legs were in the hole he was digging, and he had not been cut in half by Mr. Morgan."

Relieved, Maggie sat down cross-legged in the grass and watched "old Billy" for a while. She asked, "Why are you making that hole?"

Billy leaned on his spade and looked up at her. "To bury the silver," he said.

For some reason more than anything else that had been said or done, those four words sent fear pulsing through Maggie. She jumped up and ran as hard as she could, not caring where she went or when she stopped. As an adult, Margaret still remembered the effect the experience had on her: "I don't know how long her panic lasted, but I do recall a nightly terror that there were soldiers under her bed, with spears that might at any moment come through the mattress—*and through her!*"

The war had become much more upsetting for Maggie than it once was. Even so, she figured she was better off than the gentleman in Washington she kept hearing about. The grown-ups were always talking about how the Rebels worried "poor Mr. Linkum." Flora the cook spoke highly of Mr. Linkum, telling Maggie that he was trying to free all the "colored folks" down south. Flora's own son Charles had run away to join the Fifty-fourth Massachusetts Infantry, a regiment of free black men who fought in Mr. Linkum's army.

Maggie figured Rebels like Mr. Morgan were probably stealing Mr. Linkum's hens, or worse. After considerable thought she came up with a plan to help the poor gentleman. In *If This Be I*, Margaret described how Maggie revealed her idea one evening after supper, at a family gathering:

> Suddenly Maggie, who had curled up on the floor near Papa, spoke out: "I know what Mr. Linkum ought to do. . . . He must kill all the Rebels . . ."
>
> [Someone said,] "How shall Mr. Linkum kill them, Maggie?"
>
> Maggie, in little gasps, informed them: "On a dark, dark night, Mr. Linkum—"
>
> "It's bedtime for little girls," said Mama, softly; but Maggie stood her ground.
>
> "Mr. Linkum can take a spear—a big, long spear, maybe a mile long . . . an' then put it through all the Rebels."

At that point somebody took Maggie away, "with half of her plan for the extermination of the Confederate Army still untold."

In the end President Abraham Lincoln's troops managed to win the war without Maggie's help. On a "sweet April day" in 1865, Maggie, age eight by then, was helping Mama in the garden.

"One of the older uncles on a great gray horse . . . came galloping through the orchard," Margaret wrote later. "As he came he lifted his hat, and held it high above his head. . . . 'Lois!' he said, in a queer voice, 'Lois . . . Richmond has fallen.'"

His words meant little to Maggie, but she followed Mama and the uncle to the house, where "they told everybody that Richmond had fallen down. And for the rest of the day everybody talked and laughed, they were so happy."

After the war the residents of Maple Grove returned to their normal lives. Over the years "Maggie" became "Margaret." At age sixteen she attended Pelham Priory, an exclusive boarding school near New Rochelle, New York. When she was nineteen, she enrolled at The Cooper Union, also in New York. Later, she taught at the Girls'

Normal School (now Hunter College of the City of New York). On May 12, 1880, she married Bostonian Lorin Deland, whom she had met through his sister Emily, another teacher at the Girls' Normal School.

Lorin and Margaret lived in Boston, devoting considerable time and energy to helping unwed mothers. During four years in the early 1880s, they took at least sixty of the women into their home. There, they encouraged the women and assisted them in finding work. Margaret, who had been taught strict religious doctrines as a child, began to question some of the beliefs and attitudes that were part of her upbringing. She became particularly critical of "respectable" people who shunned young women in trouble in order to protect themselves from immorality.

As time went by, the spark of imagination that energized Maggie the child was put to good use by Margaret the adult. Her poetry and fiction appeared in such prestigious publications as *Harper's New Monthly Magazine*, *The Century*, and *The Atlantic Monthly*. She also published more than a dozen novels and novelettes between 1888 and 1932. Although she did not have any children of her own, she was praised for her portrayal of children in her work.

In *If This Be I*, Margaret expressed the distance she felt between her grown-up self and the five-year-old girl who boldly proposed marriage to an unidentified "sojer boy": "To speak frankly . . . these stories make me ask myself the startled question, 'Am I Maggie?' It is almost unbelievable to me that the anxious woman, who to-day can hardly face the miseries and sins and imbecilities of the front page of the morning paper, can be the . . . Pennsylvania imp of 1863!"

Yet after Margaret's death, *Time* magazine described her as a woman "whose fictional probing into social problems shocked her generation." Clearly the "Pennsylvania imp" was part of Margaret's spirit throughout her life.

Margaret Campbell Deland died on January 13, 1945, in Boston, about one month shy of her eighty-eighth birthday. She is buried with her husband at Forest Hills Cemetery. Her home at 35 Newbury Street is listed as a site on the Boston Women's Heritage Trail.

AND THEN THE TROUBLE BEGAN

Edwin Fitzgerald (Foy)

1856–1928

❧

In some ways Sunday, July 12, 1863, was a typical summer day in New York City. The air was hot and muggy. A few women in hoop skirts strolled along Fifth Avenue. Many of the wealthier citizens had left town for Saratoga, Newport, or Cape May. The atmosphere seemed calm, but in neighborhoods all over the city, heated discussions told a different story.

By Tuesday, July 14, New York resembled a war zone. Shouting men and women filled the streets, running, shoving, and waving weapons. Fires burned out of control. Nearly every hour brought news of grave injury or death. The madness continued into Wednesday. Downtown, people were pulled off streetcars and beaten. Houses were looted.

From his family's apartment on Eighth Avenue in Greenwich Village, seven-year-old Edwin Fitzgerald took stock of the situation. As far as he could tell, nothing was happening in his neighborhood. In spite of that his mother had forbidden him to go outside. It was too dangerous, she said. Eddie could understand why it might be best for his sisters to stay inside, but that wouldn't do for him. He had places to go.

First, he would stop at one of the water pumps scattered around Manhattan. Someone would work the long wooden handle for him,

Edwin Fitzgerald (Foy)

Reprinted with permission of the Foy family

and he would have a cool drink and refreshing face-wash all at the same time. Then he would find out what his mother was so upset about. After glancing around to see if anyone was watching him, Eddie slipped out the back door. He began to walk toward Abingdon Square.

Eight years earlier, in the spring of 1855, Richard and Ellen Fitzgerald had arrived in New York from Dublin, Ireland, with their daughter, Catherine. Relatives in the Bowery provided a place for them to live while Fitzgerald, a tailor by profession, established his business. His wife took in laundry to help make ends meet. In May a second daughter, Mary, was born. The Fitzgeralds moved into a two-story clapboard house in East Greenwich Village. There, on March 9, 1856, Edwin was born. His younger sister, Ellen, followed in 1858. Family members described Richard and Ellen Fitzgerald as loving and nurturing parents, as well as devout Catholics.

In the four decades leading up to 1860, New York's population increased sevenfold. Almost half of the more than 813,000 residents were foreign-born, mostly Irish or German. Transportation and housing shortages were among the city's most pressing problems. Overcrowded, rickety tenement buildings were a common sight. Even well-maintained buildings were located in filthy slum neighborhoods. Horse-drawn omnibuses crawled through the streets carrying as many as fifty people at a time, all crammed into a coach designed for about thirty.

The Fitzgeralds were more fortunate than many immigrants. In his book, *Clowning through Life*, Eddie Fitzgerald described his home and the times:

> [My father's tailor shop] occupied the front room of a two-story building, and we lived very comfortably in the other rooms above and back of the shop. That was an age of gorgeous clothing and lots of it. The single outfit in which a woman went on [the] street then would clothe about six women today. A woman who appeared in public without hoops looked like a collapsed umbrella, and was usually set down as belonging to the "lower clahses." The men wore flowing trousers with plaids sometimes eight inches across, and plenty of hair and whiskers. They put bear grease and pomatum on their hair then, so that thick "tidies" had to be hung on chair backs to keep them from ruining the upholstery.

In November 1860, when Abraham Lincoln was elected president of the United States, many Southern states began to discuss seceding from the Union. They weren't alone. The Democratic Party in New York had little use for Lincoln's Republican ways, and a proposal was prepared recommending that New York declare itself a "free city." When war actually broke out, however, the city aligned with the Union.

Like many other families the Fitzgeralds were caught up in the excitement. In his book Eddie wrote: "I have a dim recollection of being held up by Father or Mother at the curb to see long lines of soldiers marching down streets—probably Broadway and Fifth Avenue—with flags waving and bands playing and crowds cheering, and it all seemed very fine."

In early 1862 Eddie's father announced that he was joining the army. He probably would have been excused from service because of his wife and family, but, as Eddie put it, "Father was intensely patriotic and had the Irishman's love of a fight—and so he went."

Fitzgerald's pay as a Union soldier was $13 a month. No doubt his wife wondered how she and the children would survive on such a meager sum. Catherine left school to take a job, and even five-year-old Eddie pitched in. A friend of the family made Eddie a box and fastened a strap to it and a cleat as a rest for shoe heels. Eddie began working as a bootblack.

Two months after enlisting, Eddie's father was wounded in the shoulder and discharged. Soon after Fitzgerald returned home, his family began to realize that something else was wrong. His wife noticed "peculiarities in his conduct," Eddie wrote later. He continued: "[Father] decided one day to brighten up the front of his shop a bit. He took a pot of dark green paint . . . and began painting the window casings—but after he had finished the woodwork, he proceeded to paint the glass, too. Doctors told us that the wound in his shoulder had affected his brain. He grew worse rapidly, and the time came when we were in terror for our lives."

Richard Fitzgerald was taken to an asylum on Blackwell's Island. Eddie never saw him again. A few months after being admitted to the facility, Fitzgerald walked off the rocks into the river and drowned.

The Fitzgeralds had little money at that point and immediately moved into smaller quarters—an apartment on Eighth Avenue. According to Eddie his mother "was compelled to work at whatever she could get—washing, sewing, nursing, what not." All of the children except little Ellen had jobs. At first Eddie was permitted to shine shoes only in his own neighborhood during daylight hours. Eventually, though, he was allowed to go into other sections of the Bowery. Competition was fierce, and Eddie noticed that some of his rival bootblacks attracted business by dancing for the customers. He quickly followed suit, building a repertoire of fancy steps.

Life was difficult enough for the Fitzgeralds, but in April 1863, another tragedy struck. Four-year-old Ellen died of anemia. "There seemed no end to our troubles in those days," Eddie later wrote.

Meanwhile, the Civil War was a hot topic all over New York. Union troops had suffered a terrible defeat at Fredericksburg, Virginia. In addition, Confederate raiders such as the C.S.S. *Alabama* were making life difficult for the Union's merchant marine. Lincoln had replaced Union General George B. McClellan with Major General Ambrose E. Burnside. It was obvious that the war would not end anytime soon.

In an attempt to bolster the Union's fighting forces, the U.S. Congress had passed the first "draft law" in the nation's history: the Enrollment and Conscription Act. The law required males between the ages of twenty and forty-five to enroll. Each state had to provide a set quota of recruits. If enough volunteers could be found, that was fine, but if not, names were to be drawn from the enrollment list. The law also included a provision that an individual could avoid service by hiring a substitute or paying $300 for an exemption.

Immigrants like the Fitzgeralds had at least two problems with the enrollment act. They believed it forced poor men into battle, whereas the rich, who could afford to hire a substitute or pay the $300, sat comfortably at home. In addition, Lincoln's Emancipation Proclamation had made it clear that a Northern victory would free all slaves. It didn't take much for immigrants to become convinced that newly freed African Americans would head north in droves and take away their jobs.

Not surprisingly, the state of New York was unable to meet its recruitment quota with volunteers. A draft lottery held on Saturday, July 11, 1863, attracted a large crowd of onlookers. The police department had been informed of a plot to seize the headquarters where the lottery was being conducted, and security was heavy. Their concerns, however, appeared unfounded, as the *New York Times* reported: "The initiation of the draft on Saturday in the Ninth Congressional District was characterized by so much order and good feeling as to well nigh dispel the forebodings of tumult and violence which many entertained in connection with the enforcement of the conscription in this City."

By four o'clock that afternoon, more than a thousand names had been drawn from a large hollow wheel mounted on a stand. Names of the draftees were published in the Sunday newspaper. Drafting was scheduled to continue on Monday, July 13.

Unlike Saturday, Monday was a workday, which should have meant a smaller crowd at the draft headquarters. The group that assembled, however, was even larger than before. Instead of reporting to their jobs, hundreds of men and women marched downtown carrying NO DRAFT placards above their heads. In his memoirs Eddie Fitzgerald summed up the situation: "The Draft Boards opened their sittings, and then the trouble began."

The trouble grew more serious as the day wore on. Rioters assaulted police officers and well-dressed gentlemen. They broke into the homes of wealthy Republicans and destroyed whatever they could get their hands on. By Monday evening most of the people who had simply wanted to protest the draft had gone home. Remaining were mobs composed primarily of Irish immigrants. Their primary targets were African Americans.

Headlines in the *New York Times* on July 14 told the story: "Resistance to the Draft—Rioting and Bloodshed," "Conscription Offices Sacked and Burned," "Private Dwellings Pillaged and Fired," "An Armory and a Hotel Destroyed," "An Unoffending Black Man

Hung," "The Colored Orphan Asylum Ransacked and Burned."

On July 15, when Eddie slipped out of his family's apartment, he didn't know what he might encounter. He was a curious seven-year-old boy, accustomed to the "wild and woolly" streets of New York; however, he admitted: "[The] bullies of the Civil War period usually stayed on their own reservation. . . . The Dead Rabbits and the Bowery Boys spent most of their energy in fighting each other."

As Eddie was about to find out, the draft rioters observed no such niceties.

By Wednesday streetcars and buses had stopped running. No milk was being delivered because the milkmen were afraid to come into the city. Rioters took possession of Ninth Avenue for 10 or 15 blocks just above the Fitzgeralds' neighborhood. They cut down telegraph poles and trees and barricaded cross streets with wagons and buggies. Eddie was soon on the edge of a sea of violence.

Poor and powerless, New York's African Americans constituted a tiny percentage of the city's population. They did not pose any threat, but the mob was out of control. Eddie wrote: "From a safe distance I watched several fights—heard the yelling and saw clubs swinging and bricks and stones flying; but as soon as any shooting began, I ducked around a corner. I had no love for a gun, haven't yet, and never toted one in my life."

On Eddie's way home he noticed a "tremendous uproar" a few blocks below his house. He learned that a black man had been hanged. Once again, he was filled with curiosity. When he arrived at the scene with several other small boys, he could only stare in horror at the body dangling from a telegraph pole. Later he described his reaction: "The sight almost turned me sick, and yet it had a terrible fascination for me. I loitered about, staring at it. . . . Then a sudden revulsion overcame me and I ran home at top speed, scared and breathless."

The New York draft riots of 1863 lasted four days and left more than one hundred people dead. Soldiers were called home from the Battle of Gettysburg to help the overwhelmed New York police department quell the violence. Clergy paid a critical role by urging their parishioners to restore the peace.

Although Eddie's experience during the riots was deeply disturbing, some of the city's children fared much worse. The *New York Times* reported that ten-year-old Jane Berry was fatally injured by a bureau thrown from a window of the besieged orphan asylum and that "a boy named Kelly, aged fourteen years" suffered a gunshot wound "believed to be fatal." Also according to the newspaper, eleven-year-old William H. Thompson was killed with a bayonet.

On April 9, 1865, Confederate General Robert E. Lee surrendered to General Ulysses S. Grant at Appomattox Courthouse, Virginia. A few days later, on April 14, President Lincoln was assassinated by John Wilkes Booth. His body was carried across the country by train so that people could pay their respects. By then Eddie Fitzgerald was living in Chicago with his family and was among those who filed by the bier as it lay in state. He later wrote: "When we reached the coffin, my uncle lifted me slightly so that I could look in and see his face . . . although I was only nine, the memory has remained a vivid one to this day."

At the age of sixteen, Eddie went into show business. Deciding that "Fitzgerald" was "too Irish," he renamed himself "Eddie Foy," after an act he admired called "The Foy Sisters." Eddie Foy sang and danced in minstrel shows, clowned in circuses, and acted in Broadway productions. Married four times, he fathered eleven children. Seven of them became part of his famous vaudeville act, "Eddie Foy and the Seven Little Foys."

On February 16, 1928, Eddie suffered a heart attack and died. He was seventy-one years old.

In a eulogy at Eddie's funeral, an old friend and colleague said, "Very few people knew the real Eddie. . . . His courageous heart was a storehouse of tragedies. . . . It was the boy in Eddie Foy that kept him a boy to the end."

As a child, Eddie Fitzgerald knew the world could be a sad, painful place. He never forgot the horrors of the New York draft riots or the face of a fallen president. As an adult, he made sure people never forgot how to laugh.

A DROP OF BLOOD FOR EVERY TEAR

Ella Sheppard

1851–1914

~

In 1854 a slave named Sarah carried her three-year-old daughter, Ella, to the banks of the Cumberland River. Standing at the water's edge, Sarah forced herself to face reality: The mistress was teaching Ella to spy on her own mother. The mistress had instructed the child to tell her everything Sarah did and had started reprimanding Sarah based on Ella's innocent answers to her questions.

It did not matter that Sarah was married to Simon Sheppard, one of the many free African Americans living in Nashville, Tennessee. It was of no importance that Simon's father was a white man or that Simon had earned his freedom by working for other members of the community. Sarah was a slave, and that made her daughter one, too.

The Sheppards' first baby had died, and they had waited six years for another. Born on February 4, 1851, Samuella had been a skinny, frail infant. Sarah had prayed that the child would live, and so she had. But for what? The mistress was driving a wedge between Ella and Sarah, and Sarah was powerless to stop it.

Or was she? Sarah stared into the river's murky depths, making no effort to hold back her tears. Here was a way to end her waking nightmare and save her little girl from a life of sorrow. She stepped forward.

"Don't you do it!"

Turning, Sarah saw an older slave woman everyone called "Mammy Viney."

"Don't you do it, honey," Mammy Viney said. "Don't take what you cannot give back."

Ashamed of what she had been about to do, Sarah hugged little Ella even tighter and trudged back to her master's house. Her owners had promised Simon he could buy her for $1,300, and he was working hard to earn the money. Sarah tried to believe that everything would turn out well in the end, but still she wept, her face buried in Ella's dark hair.

One evening a few months later, Sarah overheard her master and mistress talking. The master had bought a new plantation in Mississippi and was trying to convince his wife to sell Sarah to Simon. The mistress had changed her mind.

"Sarah shall never belong to Simon," she said. "She is mine and shall die mine. Let Simon get another wife."

Sarah was horrified. The following morning, she approached her mistress.

"If you will sell Ella to her father immediately," Sarah said. "I will remain your slave. If you do not, you lose both of us. My baby shall never be a slave."

Sarah knew she could be whipped to death for speaking so boldly, but she meant what she said. She had come close to jumping into the river with her daughter once before. If necessary, she would finish the job. To her surprise the mistress accepted her offer. Sarah moved to Mississippi with her owners. Ella remained with Simon in Tennessee.

"My earliest recollection," Ella Sheppard said many years later, "was of my mother's tears over the cruelties of slavery. . . . Separation of man and wife, and parents and children, was the great torture of slavery whether masters were cruel or humane."

Three-year-old Ella did not know why her mother had gone away. Her father knew his wife's mistress would never give her up. Within two years he married Cornelia, another slave woman. He bought his new wife's freedom with the money he had saved to purchase Ella's mother. Ella got along well with her stepmother, recalling later that

Ella Sheppard Moore

Cornelia did everything for her "that [my] own mother could."

By some standards Ella led a privileged life in Nashville. Her father owned a livery stable with four carriages and eight horses. Her neighborhood playmates were the children of Nashville's free African-American elite: barbers, grocers, ministers, hack drivers, and tradesmen.

While still quite young, Ella attended a school operated by Daniel Wadkins, a free African American. Wadkins secretly taught slaves as well as free black children to read and write. To avoid detection by white authorities, he had to move his little academy from place to place. He told students to conceal their papers and books and to avoid walking in groups through the streets.

Ella had fond memories of the school even after she grew up. She wrote: "[Mr. Wadkins] used the old Webster blue back spelling book. Each class stood up against the wall, head erect, hands down, toes straight. They spelled in unison with a musical intonation, swaying their bodies from side to side, with perfect rhythmical precision on each syllable, which we thought grand. Mr. Wadkins gave out each word with such an explosive jerk of the head and spring around of the body, that it commanded our profound respect."

Ella was surrounded by educated, hardworking African Americans. Thanks to Wadkins and other dedicated teachers, a large number of free black children and adults in Nashville could read and write. Not everyone was pleased with such developments, however. In the fall of 1856, when Ella was five years old, troubling news reached the town.

In September a "vigilance committee" in Colorado County, Texas, had uncovered what they saw as an evil plot. According to the committee slaves in the area had amassed pistols, knives, guns, and ammunition, and intended to murder the entire white population. Word soon got out that the plot was widespread and that white people in all slaveholding states were in danger.

Before long Ella heard her parents and neighbors discussing accounts they had read in the local newspaper. According to the reports a slave girl in Fayette County, Tennessee, had told her owner a revolt had been organized. The master and his wife confirmed the story by eavesdropping on the slave cabins at night. In Montgomery County a keg of gunpowder was found beneath a church. Uprisings were reported in Franklin and Perry Counties.

On December 11 the Nashville *Union and American* noted: "Quite a panic has existed in parts of the State during the last two weeks growing out of some discovered plots for insurrection among the slaves."

The paper also commented that reports of slave rebellion were "exaggerated." Nevertheless, some of Nashville's working-class white citizens took the rumors very seriously. More than one hundred years later, Bobby L. Lovett described the situation in his book *The African-American History of Nashville, Tennessee:* "There was no outright race riot, but some whites kicked, beat, and physically and verbally abused Negroes along the city's streets. . . . The city imposed curfews to prevent rural slaves from coming into town. . . . The city police increased the number of patrols."

Participation in the so-called "Negro conspiracy" was punishable by imprisonment, beatings, or even death. A twelve-man vigilante committee marched into Daniel Wadkins' school and ordered him to shut down. The city council ruled that there could be "no school for Negroes free or slave taught either by white persons or blacks."

Ella could not help noticing that her father was worried. His business declined as strict codes were passed limiting the activities of African Americans. Many whites suspected free blacks of organizing revolts and accused them of setting a bad example for dissatisfied slaves. No concrete proof of a mass rebellion ever came to light, and eventually the panic subsided.

Shortly after Ella turned six, her mother came to see her. In arranging the visit Sarah's master probably thought he was doing a kindness, but, as Ella later recalled: "When [my mother] came to leave me, she found it so hard, and screamed so loud, that they said she never should see me again."

The incident saddened Ella, but there was nothing she could do. Her father's troubles seemed to be improving a little, and her life was fairly pleasant. She had no way of knowing that even more difficult times lay ahead.

On August 24, 1857, the New York branch of the Ohio Life Insurance and Trust Company failed. Soon, all across the country, banks collapsed. The nationwide depression placed Ella in grave danger. Simon Sheppard had neglected to take out manumission papers—documents required to officially free his wife and daughter. According to the law they were his property. At any moment creditors could seize

Ella and her stepmother and sell them to settle his debts. Slave prices were unusually high, putting Cornelia and Ella at even greater risk.

Before long Ella learned that her family was moving to Cincinnati. Her father wanted to make a fresh start in the free state of Ohio.

Located just across the Ohio River from the slave state of Kentucky, Cincinnati was a common stop on the "Underground Railway," a loosely organized system for helping runaway slaves escape. The city had once been home to writer Harriet Beecher Stowe, whose book about the evils of slavery, *Uncle Tom's Cabin,* had been published in 1852. One of the book's most dramatic scenes involved a young slave woman named Eliza. Feeling the same deep despair that Ella's mother, Sarah, experienced, Eliza set out across the partially frozen river, determined to carry her baby to freedom.

Abolitionists used *Uncle Tom's Cabin* to support their argument that slavery should be made illegal. Slaveholders denounced the book as false and distorted, a view disputed by Stowe in 1854 in *The Key to Uncle Tom's Cabin*. In that volume she presented the facts and documents upon which her novel was based.

Cincinnati whites were divided on the slavery issue. On one hand the city owed its prosperity to trade with slave states, and it seemed foolish to jeopardize that relationship; at the same time, a great many of the town's white citizens strongly opposed slavery and felt they should take a stand against it.

To Simon Sheppard, Cincinnati was a land of opportunity. It had a well-developed public-education system for African Americans. Blacks were allowed to testify in court. For inspiration he could look to individuals such as J. Pressley and Thomas Ball, who owned a successful photography shop, or Harry Boyd, inventor of a corded bed, who had white men working for him.

As Ella's family began to settle in, however, they quickly discovered that Cincinnati harbored a high level of racial conflict. Although African Americans lived in residential clusters scattered throughout the city, their social circles did not intersect with those of whites. Black institutions were concentrated in one section of town. A number of African Americans owned property, but their holdings were far below those of whites.

Sheppard's business got off to a slow start. As Ella later recalled, "We had literally nothing."

The family did the best they could. They collected household furniture piece by piece. Cornelia Sheppard took in washing and ironing and eventually opened a small boardinghouse. When Ella displayed musical talent, her father was able to buy her a piano and pay for lessons. But living in a free state did not guarantee equal treatment. As an African American, Ella had to meet with her music teacher in secret.

Unfortunately for Ella's health, "Ragtown"— where she and many other blacks lived—was a damp, drafty neighborhood with stinking, open drains. Ella constantly fell prey to respiratory and ear infections. When she wasn't sick, she attended Seventh Street School in Cincinnati. In his book *Dark Midnight When I Rise*, published in 2000, Andrew Ward wrote: "[Ella Sheppard] proved bright and almost agonizingly conscientious . . . a tense rail of a girl and so frail that she had to drop out for long periods. . . . She usually wore her hair in a small, tight bun that accentuated the elongated oval of her face."

In February 1861, a few days after Ella's tenth birthday, newly elected president Abraham Lincoln passed through Cincinnati on his way to Washington, D.C. Crowds gathered at the train depot to greet him. Hundreds lined the streets as he rode by in an open carriage drawn by six white horses.

Two months later, on April 12, the Confederates seized Fort Sumter in South Carolina. When President Lincoln called for volunteers to repossess the fort, some 10,000 Cincinnatians rallied to the Union cause. Others, however, chose to support the Confederacy. The recently elected mayor was an ardently pro-South Democrat. Friendships and family ties were strained to the limit and beyond.

That spring Ella noticed that every public park was filled with army recruits marching and drilling. Elderly men joined home-guard units. Boys as young as Ella tried to sign up. German, Polish, Slavic, French, and Irish regiments marched side by side. Even the "Literary Club" transformed itself into a fighting unit. The city's African-American men offered their services but were told: "Keep out of this; this is a white man's war."

Meanwhile "that human octopus" (Ella's term for slavery) continued to be a contentious subject. Whites who proclaimed allegiance to the Union were not necessarily in favor of freeing the slaves. Many feared that liberated slaves would head north, competing against whites for jobs or, failing to find work, would have to be supported at public expense. When abolitionist Wendell Phillips attempted to argue for emancipation onstage at a Cincinnati opera house, a hostile audience threw rocks and rotten eggs at him, shouting "Down with the traitor!"

In July 1862 Irish and German river workers on strike for higher wages were furious when blacks stepped forward to take the jobs at a lower pay rate. Adding to the problem was the decline of river commerce, which reduced the total number of jobs available. On July 10 a white man got into an argument with two African Americans working on the levee. The conflict escalated into a "war," in which mobs of whites roamed black neighborhoods, breaking windows and setting fires. Blacks retaliated. Guns were brandished by both sides. It took a full week for order to be restored, mainly because most of the police force was in Lexington, Kentucky, helping to defend that city against Confederate raiders.

Soon Cincinnati itself was threatened by the Confederates. In August word spread that General Kirby Smith and 1,200 Rebel raiders were headed for the town. On September 2 Mayor George Hatch placed the city under martial law under the direction of Union General Lew Wallace.

"It's fight or surrender" read a headline in the Cincinnati *Times*. "At last the Rebels are howling at our doors."

Like other African Americans eleven-year-old Ella Sheppard was worried. If the Rebels took over the town, they might capture all the blacks and force them into slavery. Kidnapping of free blacks had not been that unusual in pre-war Cincinnati, and the risks were even greater now. Cincinnati's African Americans—previously deterred from participating in the "white man's war"—suddenly found themselves in demand. They were rounded up by police and marched to the outskirts of the city to dig entrenchments. An eyewitness, Henry Howe, reported: "These helpless people were pounced upon and often bareheaded and in shirtsleeves . . . driven in squads, at the point of the bayonet. . . . Old and young, sick and well, were dragged out, and amidst shouts and jeers, marched like felons to the pen on Plum Street."

No explanation was given to the men or their families, who were naturally terrified. The captives, eventually dubbed "The Black Brigade," were put to work building military roads, digging rifle pits, chopping down trees, and constructing fortifications. Working side by side with whites, the African Americans completed their task on September 20. In the end Cincinnati was not attacked. According to General Wallace, "The enemy came and looked at [these entrenchments], and stole away in the night."

Cincinnati was threatened again on several other occasions. In each instance citizens geared up to withstand a Confederate assault. None ever occurred.

After the war was over in 1865, Ella traveled to Nashville. She spent three months with her mother, who had returned there to live. Sarah told her daughter about the incident on the banks of the Cumberland. She described the deal she had made with her mistress to ensure Ella's freedom. For perhaps the first time, Ella began to understand all her mother had endured.

In 1866 Ella's father died suddenly of cholera. Everything he had was sold to pay his debts, including Ella's piano. Just fifteen years old, Ella herself was in poor health.

"Although frail," she wrote later, "I tried every honorable opportunity to make a living. I took in washing and ironing, worked in a family, and had a few music pupils who paid me poorly. Finally I left Cincinnati and taught school in Gallatin, Tennessee."

Ella enrolled in Fisk University in Nashville in September of 1868. While there, she paid her way by teaching music, waiting tables, and washing dishes. She also played the piano and sang with a choir that eventually became the college's famous Jubilee Singers. As a member of that illustrious group, she traveled widely in America and Europe, where the choir entertained Queen Victoria of England.

At age thirty-one Ella married George W. Moore. Moore was a Fisk graduate who also earned a degree from the Theological Seminary of Oberlin College. The Moores bought a small cottage near Fisk for Ella's mother and half-sister Rosa. They also provided support for Ella's stepmother. Ella and George Moore had three children—George Sheppard, Clinton Fisk Russell, and Sarah Elizabeth. They also raised Ella's niece, Elizabeth.

Ella knew the anguish her mother had suffered most of her life, especially that day she stood on the banks of the river thinking about her child's bleak future. To Ella the Civil War was a punishment for the inhumanity of slavery. She said that God required "a drop of blood for every tear wrung from the crushed hearts and bruised bodies of our mothers."

In a eulogy following Ella's death on June 9, 1914, a former member of the Jubilee Singers company said, "Our music, inspired through her, made the hearts of others purer and better."

Ella Sheppard Moore is buried in Nashville's Old City Cemetery.

LITTLE RED CAP

Ransom Powell

1849–1899

❧

T he orders to report to Beverly, West Virginia, came as a surprise to thirteen-year-old Ransom Powell. A month earlier, when he had enlisted as a drummer boy, he had been told his unit was an independent scouting company that would remain in Hampshire and Hardy Counties. Beverly was in Randolph County. Ransom wondered if he had been told the truth in the first place, but in a way it did not matter. He would go wherever he was sent.

Born February 22, 1849, Ransom was the son of James Powell, a blacksmith, and his wife, Mary. The Powells lived in Eckhart Mines, Maryland, just across the border from West Virginia. Coal mining had put the tiny mountain village on the map. Communities all along the Potomac River relied on coal from Eckhart Mines.

When discord erupted between America's northern and southern sections in 1861, the people of Maryland were in a quandary. They lived in a slave state and seriously considered joining the Confederacy; however, they also valued their northern ties. In the end Maryland remained in the Union, but President Abraham Lincoln had to continually reassure its Southern sympathizers that he was *not* trying to abolish slavery. He also garrisoned troops in Baltimore throughout the war.

In May 1862 Ransom Powell joined the Union army. Fair-haired and blue-eyed, he had the face of a child, not a soldier. He was only

Ransom Powell

From *A History of the Coal Miners of the U.S.*, reprinted by permission of Greenwood Press

4 feet tall. On his head he wore a gold-laced cap with a crimson top.

Ransom's memoirs, written when he was twenty-six years old, do not mention what his mother and father thought about his enlisting. By the time he volunteered, the federal government had barred minors from joining the military without the consent of a parent or guardian. The Powells may have felt Ransom was old enough to participate, or Ransom may have found a way to get in without his parents' approval.

The duties of drummer boys included sounding daily calls on various percussion instruments and assisting the regimental band during ceremonies and drills. They also performed chores such as carrying water or helping the company doctor. Some learned to cut hair.

Shortly after arriving in Beverly in June, Ransom's unit was christened Company I of the Tenth West Virginia Volunteer Infantry. The regiment's main assignments were to protect the Baltimore and Ohio Railroad from Confederate attack and to ensure the safety of Union sympathizers in the area. During 1862 and 1863 the Tenth participated in numerous skirmishes and expeditions around Beverly.

In January 1864 Ransom and the other members of his regiment were quartered in a heavily timbered blockhouse about 9 miles below Petersburg, West Virginia. An unusually cold winter had set in. Temperatures were in the low twenties, trails were covered with snow and ice, and the wind was raw. There had been no major military action in the war since November. Ransom, by then fourteen years old, feared he might die of boredom.

On January 3 men from Ransom's regiment were ordered to escort a wagon train bound for New Creek. Ransom jumped at the chance to get out, in spite of the blustery weather. Years later, in his memoirs, he wrote, "I obtained permission to go with this detachment, thinking it would be a Sunday evening recreation for me."

Ransom put a few cartridges in a cap box (he was too small to carry a cartridge box) and grabbed a short-barreled rifle called a Sharp's carbine. He adjusted his cap firmly on his head and ran to join his comrades. After trudging in the snow for about a mile, the boy grew tired. One of the drivers was walking, so Ransom hopped onto the seat of his supply wagon. As he rode along, he occasionally pointed his carbine at the woods and bragged about what he would do if Rebels dared to show their faces. He was fairly certain he had nothing to fear. He was wrong.

At the junction of Moorefield Road and the Petersburg–New Creek Road, near McNemar's Church, a group of horsemen burst on the scene. They were Confederate General Thomas L. Rosser's brigade of the First Virginia Cavalry.

"Not a sound of anything could I hear from them except the clanking of swords and rattling of the horses hooves," Ransom recalled in his memoirs. "The silence was broken as soon as they came within pistol range of us."

Ransom leaped off the wagon. He and other members of his company ran halfway up a hill. Turning, they fired on their attackers. Ransom got off a few shots before heading to the woods. When he reached the crest of the hill, he encountered a Yankee.

"I observed from his movements that something was wrong," Ransom wrote later.

Looking back over his shoulder, the diminutive drummer boy saw a Rebel hot on his heels. Ransom and the other Federal soldier raised their guns. The Confederate jumped off his horse. Using the animal as a shield, he laid his revolver across the saddle and opened fire. Ransom remembered the incident vividly more than thirteen years later: "I never shall forget how near he came to shooting me. I could see where each ball would tear up the dirt around me . . . I again turned and ran, but soon heard someone laugh in my rear. I looked and saw four Rebel cavalrymen."

"Surrender," one of the Rebels ordered. He cursed then and asked, "What are you doing here?"

"Fighting for my country," Ransom replied.

"You have no country," the soldier told him.

Summoned before General Rosser, Ransom was ordered to tell how many men remained at the blockhouse. He hesitated. Rosser threatened to hang him.

"I told a tale to suit myself," Ransom recalled. "At any rate they went and captured them."

According to Captain James A. Jarboe's report, forty-two members of his company were taken prisoner that day, Ransom Powell among them. The boy who had expected to spend his years of military service in the hills near home was now on his way to Richmond, capital of the Confederacy. He had no way of knowing he was actually embarking on a much longer journey—a journey into a world more terrible than he could imagine.

The captives arrived in Richmond at night and were marched into an old tobacco house. No food was offered. Ransom's blanket was stolen. Somehow he managed to keep his crimson-topped cap, which offered at least a small amount of protection from the cold. In a few days the men were transferred to a prison on Belle Isle, located in the James River near Richmond. According to Ransom's memoirs, "They had tents for shelter, enclosed by an embankment three or four feet high. The prison was a horrible place for human beings to live in. Starvation and freezing prevailed. Death was an everyday visitor."

Fortunately for Ransom, he and several other young boys were allowed to run around freely in the enclosure. They were fed well. Their captors occasionally took them sailing or hunting. Even so, the grim realities of prison life on the damp, marshy island were constantly before their eyes. Men were beaten and shot. Vermin such as lice crawled on every available surface, inanimate or human.

In the spring of 1864, surgeon G. W. Semple inspected Belle Isle. His report dated March 6 described the devastating effects of "the crowded and necessarily filthy condition of the camp, the absence of personal cleanliness of the prisoners, the meager rations, and the effects of cold."

The Confederates began removing prisoners from Belle Isle in March. Ransom was one of the first to leave. He assumed he was going to be paroled. Instead, he learned he was being taken to a new prison camp in Sumter County, Georgia. After being given a small loaf of corn bread, the captives were marched to the train depot. Ill clad and, in many cases, barefoot, they stood shivering in the street for an hour. Ransom remembered the trip to Georgia as a slow, agonizing process. When the prisoners reached Augusta, wheelbarrows containing bacon and crackers were pushed up to the train. By then the men had been without food for two or three days.

"I enjoyed the dirty fat pieces, rind and all," Ransom wrote later in his memoirs. "[I] sucked the bone, and would fain have eaten it."

It was midnight when Ransom and his comrades entered the gates of their new home. Officially it was called Camp Sumter. Most people referred to it by the name of the nearest town: Andersonville.

Located near the Southwestern railroad tracks, Andersonville had been chosen as a prison site in November 1863. Designed to hold about 10,000 men, the stockade was 15 feet high and enclosed sixteen and a half acres of land. A small stream provided water for drinking and bathing. The camp began accepting prisoners in late February 1864.

Ransom and his comrades were the second group to arrive at the stockade. Upon seeing a large supply of timber stacked inside, they thought their situation might be somewhat better than it had been at Belle Isle. They could use the wood to build fires and keep themselves warm. Those who had blankets could make a tent, using a stick of timber as a pole.

John McElroy, a private with the Sixteenth Illinois Cavalry, entered Andersonville about two weeks before Ransom. McElroy's initial impression of the camp was relatively positive, like Ransom's. Conditions rapidly deteriorated, however, as more and more prisoners arrived. In his book, *This Was Andersonville,* published in 1879, McElroy wrote: "The fuel and building material in the Stockade were speedily exhausted. . . . The later comers had nothing whatever to build shelters with. About the middle of March . . . it began to rain. . . . It was tropical in quantity and persistency and arctic in temperature."

The administrator at Andersonville was General John H. Winder, a fifty-year-old former physician from Maryland. A close friend of Confederate President Jefferson Davis, Winder prided himself on running a tight ship. His harshest critics accused him of being a sadistic tyrant. At one point Winder reportedly bragged that he was killing off more Yankees than twenty regiments in Lee's army.

To discourage escape from the prison, Winder created a "dead line" inside the stockade, about 21 feet from the fence. It consisted of a line of posts covered by a strip of material.

"It was truly a Dead Line," Ransom wrote in his memoirs. "The offense of barely touching the Dead Line was sufficient to cause [the guards] to shoot. In many cases the only warning given was the click of the gun as the guard was preparing to fire."

In April 1864 Winder left Andersonville in the care of Henry Wirz, a native of Switzerland who had been wounded while fighting for the Louisiana Volunteers. Wirz soon acquired a reputation for cruelty rivaling that of his superior.

About a month after Wirz arrived, Ransom met one of the Confederate guards, Lewis Jones, a soldier with the Twenty-sixth Alabama Infantry. Jones got permission for the boy to stay in his quarters instead of in the stockade. In return the fifteen-year-old had to promise not to run away.

For several weeks Ransom took his meals with Lewis and four other members of the Twenty-sixth. Their rations consisted of a small amount of corn bread and bacon. The men also took Ransom hunting and fishing a few times. He attended "sham battles" staged for amusement by the Rebel regiments. The women who came to watch usually served a large dinner for the participants. Ransom was always invited.

When the Twenty-sixth Alabama was ordered to the front in May, Ransom was sad to see Jones and the others go. He feared he would be put in the stockade again. Instead he was summoned to Captain Wirz's office. For the next six weeks, Ransom lived in Wirz's house, about a mile from the prison. He ran errands for the commander and brought him his dinner each day. Occasionally he was allowed to visit his old comrades inside the camp. He became a familiar sight to the inmates. John McElroy of Illinois wrote: "We called him 'Red Cap,' from his wearing a jaunty gold-laced crimson cap. . . . No six-footer had a more soldierly heart than little Red Cap, and none was more loyal to the cause. . . . He was, beyond a doubt, the best known and most popular person in the prison."

Conditions at Andersonville continued to worsen. According to Ransom: "Wirz was a very cruel man. . . . [His wife] would laugh and jest at the Yankees dying so fast. They said they were burned out of house and home, in the state of Louisiana, by the Yankees . . . and appeared to be always seeking revenge."

The camp was enlarged to twenty-six acres in July 1864. More prisoners arrived. By August the enclosure contained more than 32,000 men. That gave each captive an average of 34 square feet in which to live and die. Plagued by disease, hunger, and lice, the inmates became, in the words of one Confederate surgeon, "a gigantic mass of human misery." In McElroy's words they comprised "a human Dead Sea, or rather a 'Dying Sea,' a putrefying stinking lake."

One day Ransom returned from running an errand to find Wirz in a particularly bad mood. The commander asked why the boy had not brought him his horse. Ransom replied that Wirz had not told him to bring her. Wirz flew into a rage and ordered a guard to put Ransom in the stockade.

"The heavy gates were opened," Ransom recalled later, "and I walked in, having breathed my last fresh air for some time. Nearly all my company had died. A great many of my old associates were gone."

Ransom adapted to life inside the prison. Whenever wagons were brought in with provisions, he climbed up on a wheel and snatched a loaf of corn bread, piece of meat, or tin of bean soup. These he shared with another prisoner, "a nice old gentleman," who cooked the food Ransom brought for both of them.

September arrived and with it, new hope. Ransom got word that a prisoner exchange had been arranged. He did not know whether to believe the news or not. Such rumors had circulated before, but Confederate and Union authorities could not seem to agree on acceptable terms for exchanging prisoners. Regardless, Ransom found out that he would be leaving Andersonville.

After two or three days on the road, Ransom and the others from the prison reached Savannah. His spirits sank as they were marched into another stockade. Resigned to the fact that he was not going to be released, Ransom soon obtained a position as a messenger. He was allowed to eat with the clerks in the commander's office. On Sunday evenings he often went to a local park—"a beautiful place with elegant fountains in it."

Within a couple of weeks, orders came that all naval prisoners on both sides of the conflict were to be exchanged. Ransom pleaded with the commanding officer to let him go but was turned down. A Yankee clerk named Mark E. Moses took pity on the drummer boy and arranged for him to pose as Walter Parsons, a cabin boy. Quite a few of the other prisoners also assumed the identities of dead or missing sailors.

As Ransom waited nervously in line, terrified of being found out, he heard a familiar voice call his name. It was the commander. In his memoirs Ransom described what happened next: "My heart was almost in my mouth. I began to think he was going to put me back into the prison. He repeated my name. I was then compelled to answer. Greatly to my surprise, he said, 'I am going to let you go home now. I know all about you being out here. When you get at home, stay there. Do not go back into the army anymore.'"

By the time Ransom reached Annapolis, Maryland, he was sick with chills and fever. He obtained a furlough and went home. Getting well took him several months and a hospital stay in Cumberland. On May 11, 1865, he was officially mustered out of military service.

Ransom found work as a coal miner. In 1870 he married Margaret Watson, called "Maggie" by her friends. Ransom and Maggie had five children: James, William, Escha May, Ransom Jr., and John.

Ransom's memoirs were first published as a series in the *Frostburg Mining Journal* between March 1875 and January 1876. Three years later, he picked up McElroy's book about Andersonville. He read with interest the lines: "I hope that if [Red Cap], or anyone who knows anything about him, sees this, he will communicate with me. There are thousands who will be glad to hear from him." Ransom did contact McElroy, and the two corresponded for a time.

In his memoirs "Red Cap" stated: "I have no doubt that I would have died if it had not been for the favors I received." He wrote to the governor of Alabama in an effort to locate Lewis Jones, the Confederate private who befriended him. It is not known if the governor ever replied.

Eventually the Powell family moved to Ohio, and in 1882 Ransom was appointed to a position in the Bureau of Pensions. Six years later he was promoted to special pension examiner.

About a month before Ransom would have turned fifty, he suffered an asthma attack complicated by pneumonia. He died at his home in Marietta, Ohio, on January 24, 1899. He is buried in the Oak Grove Cemetery in Marietta.

"I CAN AND SHALL NEVER FORGET"

Susie Baker King

1834–1912

~

O n any other spring day, the people of Savannah, Georgia, probably would have taken time to savor the fragrance of the magnolia blossoms. They might have paused to listen to the sweet song of a meadowlark. Perhaps they would have stopped to admire the dogwood trees that lined both sides of the street. Savannah, located about 12 miles from the Atlantic Ocean, was a stylish, courtly old town, built on a high bluff 40 feet above the low-water mark.

April 10, 1862, however, was not an ordinary spring day. The people of Savannah could focus on only one thing: the terrifying noise made by the giant guns. A little over a year earlier, the state of Georgia had seceded from the Union and joined the Confederate States of America. Now United States troops stationed on Tybee Island across the mouth of the Savannah River were bombarding Fort Pulaski, just 15 miles from the city itself.

On the day Fort Pulaski was attacked, many of Savannah's more than 22,000 residents gathered on their rooftops to watch, even as their windows rattled with the roar of the invader's cannons. Confederate military leaders and the vast majority of Savannah's citizens believed the elaborately designed brick stronghold was impenetrable.

Fourteen-year-old Susie Baker covered her ears as the explosions boomed overhead and jarred the earth beneath her feet. She glanced anxiously at her grandmother, Dolly Reed. Dolly's expression was grim. As one of Savannah's African Americans, Susie had been curious about and a bit afraid of the Yankees since the very beginning of the war. Some of her white neighbors had warned her about life in the North.

"Is it true the Yankees use colored slaves in place of horses, to pull their carts?" Susie had asked her grandmother.

"Certainly not," Dolly replied. "Stories like that were invented to frighten slaves and keep them from going over to the other side. The Yankees are going to set all the slaves free."

Susie was eager to see these Yankees for herself.

Although Dolly was considered a free African American, in 1862 the word *free* had a different meaning for blacks than for whites. For example, in Savannah, all "colored people," free or slave, were required to have a pass to go anywhere after nine o'clock at night. Free blacks had to have a guardian in place of a master, and restrictions were placed on social gatherings. Even free African Americans were not considered citizens and could not vote in elections. It was against the law to teach blacks, free or slave, to read or write.

Fortunately for Susie Baker, the laws were not always rigidly enforced. In 1860 there were at least six black schools in Savannah. Pupils arrived separately, pretending to be on an errand, then slipped furtively into the instructor's home. Often they wrapped their books in newspaper to conceal them. In this way Susie managed to receive a basic education. One of her teachers was her grandmother's friend Mary Woodhouse, who taught the first two years of school in her house on Bay Lane, between Habersham and Price Streets.

A quick learner, Susie continued her schooling under Mary Beasley, who told Dolly in 1860 that she had taught the twelve-year-old all she knew. During the next four months, a white friend of Susie's named Katie O'Connor gave Susie lessons each evening. (Susie had to promise not to tell Katie's father.) Finally, Susie received instruction from the landlord's son, James Blouis, a high school student. Susie

Susie Baker King

officially "graduated" from his class in the middle of 1861, when James was ordered to the battlefront with the Savannah Volunteer Guards.

Now, a year later, the war was being fought right outside Susie's door. The shelling continued all day on April 10, and on the afternoon of April 11 shots poured through the walls of Fort Pulaski. Savannah was cut off from the sea. The city of Charleston was now the only major port along the coast still held by the Confederacy.

Susie's uncle decided to put his family outside the reach of Confederate authorities by taking them to St. Catherine's Island, south of Savannah. At Dolly's request he took Susie along. From St. Catherine's they traveled to St. Simon's Island near the town of Darien, Georgia, at the mouth of the Altamaha River.

"At last, to my unbounded joy, I saw the 'Yankee,'" Susie recorded years later in her memoirs.

The fourteen-year-old girl's ability to read and write surprised the captain of the vessel that carried her to St. Simon's. He spoke to his superior, and shortly after she arrived on the island, Susie was asked to take charge of a school for former slave children. In her memoirs she wrote: "I told him I would gladly do so . . . and in a week or two I received two large boxes of books and testaments from the North. I had about forty children to teach, besides a number of adults who came to me nights."

Young Susie had to deal with many difficulties and dangers in her new life. Her teaching assignment was especially challenging because the people of the Sea Islands had been isolated from the mainland for generations and knew almost nothing about the outside world.

In addition safety was a concern. By this time all the Sea Islands were under Union control. (Confederate troops and wealthy white planters had left the islands by the spring of 1862.) Federal gunboats patrolled the coast of St. Simon's, but there were no soldiers stationed on the island to protect the men, women, and children—estimated at between 400 and 600—living in the colony. Anyone who ventured out alone at night risked being caught by Rebel raiders. The Confederate Congress had ordered that captured black civilians be returned to slavery, even if they had been set free in the past.

On two different occasions during the spring and summer of 1862, armed African-American men from the colony skirmished with Rebel troops on St. Simon's Island. In both cases Union soldiers had to be called in as reinforcements, but the bravery and determination displayed by the black civilians did not escape the notice of federal leaders. In October of that same year Union General Rufus Saxton was authorized "to raise a colored regiment." St. Simon's quickly became a military camp, where Union officers trained and drilled their unit—the First South Carolina Volunteers—to fight effectively against the Confederates.

Over the course of the war, "the First," as the unit was known to its members, was stationed in various locations in Georgia, South Carolina, and Florida. Like other African-American regiments, they were often assigned fatigue duty (routine tasks such as building roads and repairing bridges). They also raided Confederate picket posts and engaged the Rebels in combat. Black women and children traveled with the troops, serving as teachers, laundresses, cooks, and nurses. Caring for the sick and wounded took much of Susie's time.

On one occasion while nursing soldiers in a hospital in Beaufort, South Carolina, she met the founder of the American Red Cross, Clara Barton, whose dedication and bravery earned her the nickname "Angel of the Battlefield."

"Miss Barton was always very cordial toward me, and I honored her for her devotion and care to those men," Susie wrote later.

In 1862 Susie married Edward King of Darien, Georgia, a sergeant with the First. She continued to face danger daily. Disease was as serious a problem as battle injuries, and Susie's responsibilities were heavy. In her memoirs she described a smallpox outbreak: "Several cases of [smallpox] broke out among the boys, which caused some anxiety in camp. . . . Edward Davis of Company E had it very badly . . . only the doctor and camp steward, James Cummings, were allowed to see or attend him; but I went to see this man every day and nursed him. The last thing at night, I always went in to see that he was comfortable, but in spite of the good care and attention he received, he succumbed to the disease."

The young nurse did not contract smallpox because, as she later wrote, "I had been vaccinated, and I drank sassafras tea constantly, which kept my blood purged and prevented me from contracting this dread scourge."

By the time she turned fifteen, Susie was immersed in a life that would have overwhelmed many a mature adult. Even so, she took youthful pleasure in events and holidays celebrated in camp. New Year's Day, 1863, at Camp Saxton was one such occasion. Cooks labored into the night on December 31, roasting ten oxen over open fires. At about ten o'clock in the morning the next day, people began arriving on steamboats. A program of music and speaking took place in a grove of live-oak trees adjoining the camp, and Abraham Lincoln's Emancipation Proclamation was read aloud. The troops participated in a dress parade.

Charlotte L. Forten, an African-American educator who had moved to the area from Pennsylvania, recorded her impressions in her journal: "It was a brilliant sight—the long line of men in their brilliant uniforms, with bayonets gleaming in the sunlight. . . . To me it was a grand triumph, that black regiment doing itself honor in the sight of white officers, many of whom, doubtless, 'came to scoff.'"

Susie described the event as "a glorious day for us all," adding, "We enjoyed every minute of it." Colonel Thomas Wentworth Higginson, one of the white officers in command of the First, was impressed by Susie's many abilities. He wrote in his journal: "I have never in my life seen dancing so perfectly graceful as that of our Commissary Sergeant . . . with Mrs. King, one of the laundresses, a little jet black woman who can read and write and has taught a little school."

Everyday life in camp was pleasant in some ways. Camp food was simple but usually adequate. Once in awhile fresh beef was available. Other menu items included soup with dried, pressed vegetables in it; salt beef; and hardtack (a thick, hard cracker made of flour, water, and salt). Coffee and tea were popular beverages. In a letter to his wife, Colonel Higginson described the scene at Camp Saxton in February of 1863: "Grass is growing green, jasmine twine and blossom in the tree tops and fill my tent with fragrance, peas are two inches high on some of the islands, and it is as raw and chilly a day as one could desire to shiver in."

During her stay on the island, Susie lived in a tent much of the time. In winter, when it was very cold, she often put a little earth in the bottom of an iron mess pan, filled it with coals from the cook shed, and carried it back to her tent, where she covered it with another pan. "In this way," she wrote, "I was heated and kept very warm."

Although she worked hard and took her responsibilities seriously, Susie's youthful impulsiveness and inexperience sometimes got her into trouble. One incident occurred shortly after the regiment was transferred from Camp Saxton, 2 miles from Beaufort, to Seabrooke, about 10 miles away. Susie and her friend Mary Shaw decided to retrieve a few items Susie had left with a neighbor who lived just outside Camp Saxton. They rode the commissary wagon into Beaufort and walked to their former neighbor's house. Unfortunately, they returned to Beaufort too late to catch the wagon back to Seabrooke.

Both girls had relatives in Beaufort, but they decided they did not want to spend the night there. Certain they could reach Seabrooke before dark, they started walking. Susie described the episode in her memoirs: "We had not gone many miles, however, before we were all tired out and began to regret our undertaking . . . we grew more frightened, fearful of meeting some animal or of treading on a snake. . . . Our feet were so sore we could hardly walk. . . . We had gone about six miles when night overtook us. There we were, nothing around us but dense woods, and as there was no house or any place to stop at, there was nothing for us to do but continue on. We were afraid to speak to each other."

Not long before midnight Susie and Mary arrived at Seabrooke, but they couldn't relax just yet. They knew they would be stopped by a sentry, and they had no idea what the current password was.

"Who comes there?" demanded a guard.

"A friend without a countersign." Susie replied in a quavering voice. She held her breath. To the girls' immense relief, the sentry approached and recognized them. They were admitted into the lines.

During the weeks and months that followed, Susie and Mary were teased and jokingly called "deserters." Susie laughed along with the men, but she did not undertake such a journey again.

In addition to tackling nursing and teaching chores, Susie served as a camp laundress. She also learned to shoot a musket, often hitting the target. "I assisted in cleaning the guns and used to fire them off to see if the cartridges were dry," she wrote later. "I thought this great fun. I was also able to take a gun all apart, and put it together again."

Although Susie enjoyed assembling weapons, knowing they would be used against humans troubled her deeply. Nevertheless, she eventually became toughened against the horrors of war. As an adult she was able to look back and describe the experience objectively: "It seems strange how our aversion to seeing suffering is overcome in war—how we are able to see the most sickening sight . . . without a shudder; and instead of turning away, how we hurry to assist in alleviating their pain, bind up their wounds, and press the cool water to their parched lips, with feelings only of sympathy and pity."

During the federal bombardment of Charleston in the summer of 1863, Susie often climbed onto the ramparts at Fort Wagner to watch. On the path to the fort lay the skulls of men who had died there during battles earlier in the war. Susie had to move the skulls to one side in order to pass. By that time such a grim task did not disturb her for, as she later noted, "They were a gruesome sight . . . but . . . I had become accustomed to worse things."

In February 1864 the regiment received a new name: The Thirty-third United States Colored Troops. That summer, joined by two other regiments, the Thirty-third attacked Fort Gregg on James Island. As the wounded were brought into camp, Susie had to call upon her creative cooking skills. "I had a few cans of condensed milk and some turtle eggs," she wrote, "so I thought I would try to make some custard. . . . This I carried to the men, who enjoyed it very much."

After the war Susie and Edward King returned to Savannah, where Susie opened a school in her home. For about a year she taught twenty children, receiving $1.00 a month for each pupil. In 1866 Susie and Edward were looking forward to the birth of their own child when tragedy struck. While working as a longshoreman, loading and unloading ships, Edward fell and hit his head. He did not recover.

"My husband, Sergeant King, died," Susie wrote, "leaving me soon to welcome a little stranger alone."

Over the next several years Susie continued to teach and also worked as a laundress and cook for a wealthy family. She moved to Boston, where she played an active role in the Women's Relief Corps, auxiliary to the Grand Army of the Republic, a Union veterans' organization. In 1879 she married Russell L. Taylor. Susie's son, who had become an actor, died in Shreveport, Louisiana, in 1898.

What Susie witnessed as a child still haunted her at age fifty-four, when she wrote:

> I can and shall never forget that terrible war until my eyes close in death. The scenes are just as fresh in my mind to-day as in '61. I see now each scene—the roll-call, the drum tap, "lights out," the call at night when there was danger from the enemy, the double force of pickets, the cold and rain. How anxious I would be, not knowing what would happen before morning!
>
> There are many people who do not know what some of the colored women did during the war. There were hundreds of them who assisted the Union soldiers by hiding them and helping them to escape. . . . These things should be kept in history before the people.

In 1912, ten years after writing her memoirs, Susie Baker King Taylor died at age sixty-one in a rented room in the Boston area. She is buried next to Russell Taylor in Roslindale, Massachusetts.

BOUND TO GO

Elisha Stockwell Jr.

1846–1935

~

I n September 1861 Elisha Stockwell Jr. of Alma, Wisconsin, heard
United States army recruiters were taking applications at the
town's log schoolhouse. He responded without hesitation. Although he was only fifteen years old and small for his age, he could,
in his words, "rake and bind and keep up with the men." Never mind
that a man's wage was $1.00 a day and Elisha was paid only 50 cents.
He knew he was old enough to be a soldier, and he wanted to defend
his country.

The United States was at war with eleven Southern states known
officially as the Confederate States of America. On April 12 Confederates had attacked Fort Sumter in South Carolina, seizing it from
U.S. troops. On July 21 the Confederate army had defeated Union
forces at Manassas Junction, Virginia.

Filled with patriotic pride, Elisha joined his friends and relatives
at the schoolhouse that September afternoon and added his name to
the list of volunteers. A moment later, humiliation replaced pride as
his father scratched through the signature. Elisha was too young to
go to war, he stated. Elisha's older sister, Adelaide, scolded him for
even thinking he could be a soldier. "You're just a little snotty boy,"
she said.

At the same meeting Elisha's friend Edgar Houghton also signed
up to serve. Edgar was just sixteen, but no one objected. As Elisha

watched his own father cross his name off the list, he vowed to prove to everyone that he was as much of a man as Edgar.

"I am not the little boy you think I am," he told his family.

Later that fall, Elisha's father accepted a contract to burn charcoal. Elisha was to divide his time between school and the coal pit. One day in February 1862, the fifteen year old took his father's oxcart from the pit into Alma for supplies. While he was there, he learned that Edgar's father, who had also enlisted in September, was home on furlough. Elisha went to see him.

"Take me back to camp with you when you go," he requested.

David Houghton hesitated. "Has your father consented?" he asked. "You know, if you go without his permission, he can come and take you out."

"I'm bound to go," Elisha told him. "If you won't help me get to Fond du Lac, I'll go alone—on foot. I can't afford the railway fare."

Houghton saw nothing but determination in the boy's expression. Fond du Lac was clear on the other side of the state.

"All right . . . I'll see you through. Be at the hotel in Black River Falls on Sunday at noon," Houghton responded.

A load of coal was scheduled for delivery to Black River Falls that weekend, and Elisha volunteered to take it. He told his father he would like to stay in town and attend a dance on Sunday night. He would have dinner with Adelaide and her husband, Nicholas Gervais, who lived in Black River Falls.

Elisha Stockwell Jr. never forgot the events of that Sunday. Sixty-five years later, in 1927, his children encouraged him to put his experiences on paper. By then cataracts had robbed him of his sight, so he used a piece of wood to guide his writing, turning the wood over to start each new line. Concerning that day in February 1862, he wrote: "I unloaded [the coal] at the blacksmith shop, drove up to my brother-in-law's, tied the oxen to the fence, and went in and saw my sister a few minutes. I told her I had to go down town. She said, 'Hurry back, for dinner will soon be ready.'"

Two years passed before Adelaide saw her little brother again.

At the army camp near Fond du Lac, Elisha joined Company I of

Elisha Stockwell Jr. in 1864.

the Fourteenth Wisconsin Volunteer Infantry. He said he didn't know how old he was but thought he was eighteen. The recruiting officer estimated his height at 5 feet, 5 inches.

"I wasn't that tall two years later when I re-enlisted, but they let it go," Elisha recalled.

Before the end of February, the blue-eyed, sandy-haired "little snotty boy" wore a dark blue uniform and carried a gun. One of the other soldiers, a big, husky fellow called "Curly," was not impressed with the newly created "Private Stockwell."

"I test all recruits to see if they can fight," Curly informed the boy. With that, he began to cuff him around, shoving and pushing until Elisha told him he had had enough.

"I didn't enlist to fight that way," he told Curly. "But if you'll get your gun and go outside the camp with me, I think I can convince you that I can shoot as well as you can."

Curly never bothered him again.

As a member of a group of new recruits called "the awkward squad," Elisha quickly adapted to life in camp. He learned the fundamentals: how to stand erect; face left or right; salute; march forward, to the rear, by the flank, and sideways; shift arms to various positions; load his gun; fire in standing, kneeling, and prone positions; and how to parry and thrust with his bayonet.

While in camp at Fond du Lac, the troops lived in Sibley tents, which consisted of a large canvas cone that peaked about 12 feet from the ground. A center pole on a tripod provided support and allowed the men to tighten or loosen the tension of the canvas. The layer of straw Elisha slept on was a poor substitute for his bed back home, but he considered it "quite comfortable."

The boy from Alma was something of a "sleepyhead," a fact that gave his mother serious concerns about how he would fare in the army. On one occasion when he was called to guard duty during the night, he responded as if awake but continued sleeping. The sergeant jerked him out of bed by his hair. Elisha reported to his post, but when he got up the next morning, he had no idea why his head was so sore.

In March 1862 the Fourteenth Wisconsin Volunteer Infantry left Fond du Lac and traveled by train to Benton Barracks in St. Louis, Missouri. By then Elisha was fairly certain he was far enough from home that his father couldn't come after him, so he wrote to his family. A letter headed "St. Louis, March 12, 1862," read: "Respected parents, I take my pen in hand to let you know that I am well and where I am. . . . We are about 5 miles from the Mississippi River at Benton barracks. . . . We marched through Schoggo [Chicago] the mud was over shoe all of the way through. . . . Well, I must hold on for they are agoing to drilling so goodby for just now."

On March 30 he wrote: "Dear Mother . . . We are at Savannah [Tennessee] now. . . . I stood picket guard last night. . . . There is a good many peach trees here and they are all in bloom. . . . How does Frank [Elisha's younger brother, born in 1849] get along? What is Miss Pomroy a doing? I would like to get hold of one of Miss Pomroy's pies."

Instead of Miss Pomroy's pies, Elisha had to content himself with hardtack, a flour-and-water cracker or biscuit about 3 inches square and half an inch thick. Although many soldiers complained about these "teeth dullers," and some suggested building fortifications with them, Elisha liked hardtack and "never got tired of it."

On the afternoon of April 6, 1862, the Fourteenth was ordered to Pittsburg Landing, Tennessee, to join forces with General Ulysses S. Grant's Army of the West Tennessee. Although most of Elisha's comrades cheered the news, he didn't share their enthusiasm.

"I felt I would just as soon stay where we were," he later wrote.

At eleven o'clock that night, the Fourteenth arrived by boat at Pittsburg Landing. Earlier that day Confederate troops led by General Albert S. Johnston had surprised the Federals, capturing a Union camp. The Federals had fought savagely with Johnston's forces near Shiloh Church, and casualties on both sides had been appalling. Johnston had been killed. The day had ended with the Federals repulsing a Confederate charge. At that point Union gunboats had taken over, firing on the woods beyond Grant's line.

That night, according to Grant's personal memoirs, the rain "fell in torrents and our troops were exposed to the storm without shelter." Elisha slept standing up, his bayonet stuck in the ground, his chin resting on the butt of his gun, a blanket draped across his shoulders. As miserable as the night of April 6 was, it would seem like pure pleasure to him before the next day was over.

"The first dead man we saw was a short distance from the clearing," Elisha recorded in his memoirs. "I didn't look at him the second time as it made me deathly sick."

More than sixty years after the experience, he vividly remembered the details of the man's hideous injuries. Nearly all the members of the regiment "were pale as ghosts." Of that same incident Elisha's friend Edgar Houghton later wrote: " . . . the thought uppermost in our minds was that we too might be numbered with the slain before the setting of the sun."

On their way to the front, Elisha and his comrades saw what some of the gunboat shells fired the night before had done: "The Rebs had taken possession of a camp that belonged to our troops. . . . There were four of them playing cards, and all of them were dead. Each had three cards in his left hand and the four cards lay in the middle of the blanket. The tent was blown to atoms."

The men of the Fourteenth made their way through a wooded area, stepping over and around the bodies of soldiers who had fallen the day before. Company I was formed into a line and ordered to lie down. Big, tough Curly, who had boxed the new recruits' ears at Fond du Lac, lay to Elisha's right. Elisha noticed that Curly "stuck his nose into the mud the same as the rest of us."

As the shells flew over him, Elisha contemplated the choices he had made: "I thought what a foolish boy I was to run away to get into such a mess as I was in. I would have been glad to have seen my father coming after me."

When his unit was ordered to advance, Elisha tried to put his fears aside. He went forward with a will, certain his regiment "would do them up in a hurry and have this over with." As he ran downhill, a bayonet poked him in the back. He turned around to tell the soldier behind him to be more careful. To his horror he realized the man had been shot in the forehead.

"We had lost all formation, and were rushing down the road like a mob," Elisha wrote later. "When we got to the foot of the hill . . . I got behind a small tree."

He couldn't see "the Rebs" because of the thick brush, so he fired at puffs of smoke coming from the top of the next hill. Suddenly "a grape shot came through the tree and knocked me flat . . . I thought my arm was gone . . . I got to my feet."

Suddenly a swarm of Confederates charged downhill toward Elisha. He looked back to check on the rest of his unit and "saw the colors going out of sight over the hill." Only two men from his regiment were still visible. Elisha started to run. In his memoirs he described what happened next: "At that instant the bullet cut across my right shoulder, and it burned like a red hot iron. My first thought was my clothes were afire . . . I began to realize that the Rebs were shooting at me. . . . The ground looked queer, as though it was boiling."

As Elisha stumbled to his place in the ranks, his left arm began to throb. He tried to raise it but couldn't. A lieutenant noticed the boy was injured. He told Elisha to get behind a tree or stump until they made their next charge and then go to the Landing.

"I was as tickled as a boy let out of school," Elisha wrote later.

During the weeks and months that followed, however, the school of war was in session—and the lessons were hard.

Disease killed more men than battle. David Houghton, the man who had brought Elisha to Fond du Lac, contracted typhoid fever and died in May. Houghton's son Edgar, who had cared for his father in the hospital, caught the fever and was sent away to recover. He eventually returned to the unit. Elisha recalled: "We heard the 'Dead March' now nearly every day, and I thought that the most solemn music I ever heard. It was played on muffled drum and fife. They nailed rough board boxes together to bury the dead in."

Elisha himself remained healthy for the time being. In October a boil on the instep of his left foot kept him out of the action at Corinth, Mississippi, where a fierce hour-long battle left thousands of Federal and Confederate soldiers wounded or dead. The encounter ended in a Union victory. Finally able to wear his left shoe, Elisha marched with his company along a road "lined with the dead on both sides . . . some places very thick and mostly Rebs." He described it as "the most horrible fifteen miles I ever marched."

After pursuing the retreating Confederates for two days, his regiment headed back to Corinth in a chilly, drizzly rain. Sleeping in wet clothes on the soaked ground took its toll. A few days later, shaking and feverish, Elisha fainted during dress parade. He recovered, but for the remainder of his service in the army and nearly a year after he got home, he experienced the same severe symptoms every time he caught a cold.

In May 1863 the Fourteenth joined Union troops around Vicksburg, Mississippi. Elisha remembered soldiers on both sides climbing up on the breastworks at night to talk, joke, and sing songs for an hour at a time. At one point a group of "Rebs" even came across the line for a cup of coffee.

On June 25 the Federals set off more than 2,000 pounds of powder under the Confederate works at Vicksburg, then began firing. The Fourth of July, a day on which Americans normally celebrated independence, took on a very different meaning for Confederates in 1863. The date became associated not only with the loss of Vicksburg but with the defeat of Confederate troops at Gettysburg, Pennsylvania.

Elisha's regiment was one of those that took possession of Vicksburg. In a letter to his mother headed "In Camp Near Vicksburg, July 8th, 1863," he wrote: "We marched down on main street in front of the court house and gave three cheers for the flag of our union. . . . It was the happiest fourth [of July] that I ever spent. . . . As soon as I get a chance I am going to get my picture taken and send it home."

In January 1864 Elisha went back to Alma with his regiment for a thirty-day furlough. Before half the time had passed, he was ordered to Milwaukee. There, his furlough was extended twice, and he was offered a job as an office boy. He declined but made an offer of his own to a fifteen-year-old girl he had met in Milwaukee: Catherine Agnes Hurley. She accepted, and they were married on March 14.

At the end of his original three-year tour of duty, Elisha reenlisted in the Union army. He served until the end of the war, when he was mustered out with the rest of his company as "Corporal Stockwell." Elisha and Catherine raised eleven children and lived, at various times, in Wisconsin, Minnesota, and North Dakota.

In 1927, more than sixty years after a worried mother's "sleepyhead" set out to prove that he was not a "little, snotty boy," a man in the twilight of his life committed his Civil War memories to paper. He closed with this statement: "This ends my experience. I haven't told all, but what I have is the truth to the best of my recollections."

Elisha Stockwell Jr. died in 1935 at the age of eighty-nine in Beach, North Dakota, where he and his wife had settled in 1906.

A STRAW TO HOLD

John Henry Crowder

1846–1863

❧

Shortly after John Henry Crowder was born, his father, Jacob, went off to Mexico with the United States Army. He never returned. In 1848, after divorcing Crowder, John's mother, Martha Ann Spencer, left Kentucky with her two-year-old son and moved to New Orleans. She had friends there—free African Americans like herself—and she looked forward to a new life.

By 1850 New Orleans, Louisiana, was the fifth-largest city in the United States and home to more than 116,000 people. Nearly 10,000 were free people of color. Unlike free blacks in other southern states, those in Louisiana could travel without restriction and even testify against whites in court. Many of them owned property; some even owned plantations and slaves. Quite a few were well educated. Most had jobs as carpenters, mechanics, cooks, and the like.

Slaves who lived in New Orleans also had opportunities not available to their counterparts in the rural South. Although most were unskilled laborers owned by businesses and institutions, many were encouraged to learn a trade such as bricklaying, painting, or cabinetmaking. Some were trained as porters, shoemakers, or blacksmiths.

Too young to remember much about his Kentucky birthplace, John quickly got to know his new hometown. New Orleans was a place of intriguing contrasts, from an untamed swamp where alligators thrived to the highly civilized St. Charles Hotel. And of course there was the rolling Mississippi River, sweeping past the city in a huge curve. Steamships, sailboats, and barges brought the world to John's doorstep, sometimes docking three or four deep at the piers.

When John was eight years old, he signed on as a steamboat cabin boy. Every month he gave his meager pay to his mother to supplement the money she made by taking in sewing. Although his mother had remarried in 1850, her new husband, Thomas Stars, was not much help. Friends of the family described him as "a worthless, trifling fellow" who "wastefully squandered in drink and drunkenness the small earnings that [Martha Ann] had earned."

Young John did not have much time for play, but now and then special events gave him a chance to be a child. One such occasion occurred each January when the whole town celebrated the Battle of New Orleans. Back in 1815, British troops had tried to capture the city, then were defeated by a unique assortment of African Americans, Anglo Americans, Creoles, foreigners, frontiersmen from Tennessee and Kentucky, Native Americans, pirates, and Santo Domingans. Each year, on the anniversary of the battle, all the veterans paraded through town. John always felt proud to see African Americans marching with the rest of the men as the band played and the crowd cheered.

John continued to work hard. When he was twelve, he was promoted to steamship steward, earning considerably more than what he had made as a cabin boy. That money, too, went to his mother. Although John did not attend school, he did receive an education, thanks to Reverend John Mifflin Brown, an old friend of his mother's.

Brown, a brilliant African American, believed a person should be encouraged to grow spiritually and mentally no matter what the color of his skin. He had been arrested more than once because he refused to prohibit slaves from attending his church services. He took a special interest in John, teaching him at every opportunity.

Meanwhile, events occurred that were far more significant than any one person's salary or education. In November 1860 Abraham Lincoln—who had not even been included on the ballot in Louisiana—was elected president of the United States. Two months later, Louisiana withdrew from the Union. By early February 1861 a total of seven states had seceded. All across the South people celebrated the birth of what they considered a new nation: the Confederate States of America.

In an editorial dated April 17, 1861, the *Daily Picayune,* a New Orleans newspaper, called Lincoln's administration a "dictatorship." The editorial commented sarcastically that Lincoln and his supporters considered the Union "legally unbroken, and the seven States . . . only temporarily absent without leave from Congress."

Everyone knew, however, that the situation was much more serious. Just four days earlier, the Union army had surrendered Fort Sumter to the Confederates. War could no longer be avoided. The free African-American men of New Orleans stepped forward to offer their services, as they had so often in the past. Like most Southerners they were determined to protect their families and homes from attack. In addition, by rallying to the Confederate cause, they hoped to raise their stature in the eyes of local whites.

The *Daily Picayune* greeted the actions of the free blacks with enthusiasm. An article published on April 21, 1861, reported: "Tomorrow evening, the most respectable portion of the colored population of the city will hold a meeting at the corner of Greatmen and Union streets, for the purpose of organizing companies among themselves . . . to help repel any enemy who may invade the soil of Louisiana."

The free men of color—most of whom were literate individuals of mixed black and white ancestry—formed a regiment called the Native Guards. On November 23 nearly 1,500 took part in a grand parade, "by far the greatest and most imposing sight ever presented by the population of the Crescent City," according to the *Daily Picayune.* The African-American soldiers who marched that day were not the elderly veterans of the War of 1812, who had ridden in carriages in the last parade. The Native Guards were young and vigorous, the best and brightest of the free African-American community.

In March 1862 Governor Thomas D. Moore accepted the all-black regiment into the Louisiana militia. Its line officers received commissions; however, the men were not given uniforms or guns and did not drill with white units. African Americans had participated in the military defense of New Orleans for more than one hundred years, but this new conflict was different. Many Southerners feared that black soldiers might try to liberate the slaves or encourage them to rebel.

By this time John was working as a porter for a jewelry store. His pay was more than he had received as a steamboat steward, but he was dissatisfied. It seemed to him that he should be doing more to take care of his mother.

When Union forces captured New Orleans in April 1862, Southern troops fled the city—with the exception of the Native Guards. Concealing the weapons they had managed to obtain, they returned home to their families. The pressure to take a stand for the Confederacy had vanished along with the Rebel soldiers.

Before long most of the free men of color came forward again, this time to offer their services to the Federals. Union General Benjamin F. Butler wondered why the African Americans had enlisted in the Confederate army in the first place. Native Guards member Charles W. Gibson explained that their goal had been to protect their property, rights, and families. Refusal to cooperate could have resulted in injury or even death.

That made sense to Butler, but he was still not ready to enlist blacks, free or slave. For one thing he was not convinced that African Americans were suited for military service. Like many whites he suspected that blacks would not fight if sent into battle. In addition, President Lincoln had expressed concern that such a move would incite the border states of Missouri, Maryland, and Kentucky to withdraw from the Union.

In August 1862 Butler was forced to reconsider his views. Confederate General John C. Breckinridge's troops nearly overpowered Butler's men, many of whom were weakened by sickness. Efforts to recruit enough white Louisianans to fill the Union army's needs had been disappointing, and Butler had been told not to expect reinforcements. Warned that the Rebels were planning to recapture New Orleans, he wrote a letter to Union Secretary of War Edwin M. Stanton.

"I shall call on Africa to intervene," Butler declared, "and I do not think I shall call in vain."

When the letter was publicized in a New Orleans newspaper, most of the white citizens were horrified. The *Daily Picayune,* which had heaped praise on Louisiana's black soldiers in years past, did a complete about-face. The editorial page now claimed that "the unfitness of the [African American] for military service and duty is known to everybody."

Ignoring the opposition, Butler issued an appeal for men of color to join the Union army. By December 1862 three regiments had been filled. Although other African-American regiments were formed during the war, only the Louisiana Native Guards had black commissioned officers. Averaging thirty years of age, they were educated, sophisticated men. Some had served as officers in the Mexican army. Among them was sixteen-year-old Second Lieutenant John Henry Crowder.

A woman named Maria Wilson met John when she was visiting her son in camp near New Orleans. Noticing the "very bright and interesting youth," she asked, "For God's sake, what are you doing here?" John answered that he wanted to serve his country and that his mother was very poor, and he had to do something for her support. The woman eventually became a close friend of John's mother.

John had received his lieutenancy because of his intelligence and ability, including the ability to lie about his age. He was well aware that commissioned officers were supposed to be at least eighteen, but he figured no one had to know. In a letter to his mother written shortly after enlisting, he mused: "If Abraham Lincoln knew that a colored lad of my age could command a company, what would he say?"

What white soldiers said about African-American officers was not encouraging. One lieutenant complained to a newspaper reporter that it was humiliating for him to obey a black officer. A brigadier general asserted, "With existing prejudices, few or no good white officers will enter a regiment with colored officers."

Meanwhile, John Crowder was dealing with other problems. In a letter to his mother dated November 20, 1862, he denied rumors that he had been arrested and had caused the death of a sergeant:

> [Sergeant François] was my warmest friend . . . and I was not the one that caused his death so help me God. It has also been said that I was married and I was cashiered for marrying a Contraband. I am neither married nor have been cashiered. . . . P.S.: Please give my love to . . . my God daughter Little Frank. Accept my love yourself. I now close my letter hungry and remain
>
> Your son as before,
John H. Crowder

In mid-December 1862 Butler was replaced by General Nathaniel P. Banks, who had a history of opposition to the enlistment of black soldiers. Not long after taking command, he advised a group of free African-American officers that if they had complaints about how they were treated, they should resign. The men complied within weeks, stating, "We did not expect, or demand, to be put on a perfect equality in a social point of view with the whites. But we did most certainly expect the privileges, and respect due to a soldier who had offered his service and his life to his government, ever ready and willing to share the common dangers of the battlefield. This we have not received."

Well aware that Banks was getting rid of black officers, John vowed to his mother that he would "stay in the service, as long as there is a straw to hold to . . . I do not intend to resign, nor will I resign unless I am the only black officer in the service."

For several months John's regiment was headquartered at Lafourche Crossing and assigned to guard the New Orleans, Opelousas, and Great Western Railroad. In January 1863 the First Louisiana Native Guards were stationed at Fort St. Leon on the west bank of the Mississippi River, about 15 miles below New Orleans. In a letter dated January 2, John defended himself against accusations of drunkenness and smoking:

"Mother I have done everything that I promised you to do. I do not smoke nor drink liquor and you know it. . . . You make it the first thing to write to me of when you are angry. You say that I do not care for you . . . and you know that I love you and yet you say that I do not."

In March the Native Guards were sent to Baton Rouge. John's troubles continued. On April 18, 1863, he wrote his mother that he had been sick "with a severe cold and a burning fever." While he was sick, an older woman named Mrs. Marsh nursed him back to health, treating him as if he were her own son. Her behavior irritated another black officer, a Captain Lewis, who resented the special care she was giving John.

Later, after John had recovered, he learned from Mrs. Marsh's husband that a man in John's regiment had "made signs at the lady of the most disrespectful kind." John had the soldier arrested.

"I remember your first lesson," he wrote his mother. "That was to respect all females."

John's act of chivalry angered Captain Lewis, who had witnessed the man's behavior toward Mrs. Marsh but had done nothing about it. John's actions made Lewis seem derelict in his duties. The captain threatened to get John thrown out of the army for being underage.

On May 1 John, now seventeen, finally had good news to report: "Today the paymaster has commenced to pay us off," he wrote. "We will be paid for five months."

He sent $250 with a note to his mother on May 4. The next day he wrote again, asking her to let him know if she received the money. "Let me hear from you soon as possible," he finished. "My love to all friends and yourself. Goodbye. I am Your Affectionate Son, John H. Crowder."

In mid-May 1863 the First and Third Regiments of the Native Guards tramped down hot, dusty roads to Port Hudson, Louisiana. There, on May 23, they joined other Federal troops to wage an assault. The stakes were high for both North and South. If the Union could take Port Hudson and Vicksburg, another Mississippi River stronghold, the Confederacy would be cut in two. Confederate military forces would be separated. Transportation of vital supplies would become highly difficult, if not impossible.

Like Vicksburg, Port Hudson was extremely well fortified. Situated on 80-foot-high bluffs overlooking the river and protected by forests and natural ravines, it seemed impregnable. And no one doubted that the Confederates would attempt to hold it at all costs.

Aided by Union admiral David Farragut's warships, General Banks planned to bombard the Rebels for several hours, then send his ground troops rushing in all at once. The Native Guards were ordered to the extreme right of the Union line, straddling the Telegraph Road that ran along the river. Parallel to that road the Confederates had dug a series of rifle pits.

John and the other Native Guards prepared themselves to prove that they could and would fight. Union brigadier general William Dwight Jr. was eager to help them in this effort. The thirty-one-year-old Dwight had been placed in charge of the African-American regiments at Port Hudson. He decided the upcoming assault was the perfect opportunity to test the resolve of the black soldiers.

"I am going to storm a detached work with them," he wrote in a letter to his mother. "I shall compromise nothing in making this attack, for I regard it as an experiment."

On Wednesday morning, May 27, Dwight ordered the Native Guards to advance. They crossed a creek called the Big Sandy and formed a line of battle in a grove of willow trees just south of the Telegraph Road. They were 600 yards from the main Confederate position. The moment of truth had arrived. At about ten o'clock they emerged from the woods into the oppressive heat. Moving at a double-quick, they covered 100 yards, then 200 . . .

Suddenly the Confederates opened up. John and his comrades found themselves in a whirlwind of shot and shell. Pieces of railroad iron, some nearly 2 feet long, flew among them—and into them. They were under attack from three sides, targeted by men in the rifle pits as well as those behind the breastworks and others shooting from a separate battery out on the water. The Guards fired a single volley in response, then fell back in confusion. As they ran for the willow grove, the Confederates mowed them down.

According to some accounts the Native Guards charged again at least three and perhaps as many as six times. Other reports indicate that they continued to exchange fire from the woods but did not attempt another run at the fortress. In any case their actions did not achieve the desired result; in fact, none of the Union regiments succeeded that day in their assault against Port Hudson. Even so, Northern newspapers were filled with praise for the now tried-and-proven black troops. Banks was thrilled.

"They fought splendidly! splendidly!" he enthused in a letter to his wife. "Their charges upon the rebel works . . . exhibited the greatest bravery."

Second Lieutenant John Crowder never got to hear the glowing tributes. He lay dead on the field of battle.

After Port Hudson, Banks began to aggressively recruit African-American soldiers. At the same time he continued to apply pressure on black officers to step down. He considered their presence to be a "constant embarrassment and annoyance." Most of the officers who withstood Banks's machinations resigned anyway in the face of overwhelming prejudice and disrespect from white soldiers.

John Crowder was buried in a pauper's grave not long after the May 27 assault. After the war Thomas Stars left New Orleans, and John's mother began her own battle with the United States government. Declaring that her son had provided much of her support, she requested a dependent's pension. Testifying on her behalf was Reverend John Mifflin Brown, who had become a bishop in the African Methodist Episcopal Church and a trustee of Howard University. Finally, in 1874, the Pension Office began sending Martha Ann Stars a stipend of $12 per month. The payments ended with her death in May 1900.

"I WANTED TO FIGHT TO MUSIC"

Opie Percival Read

1852–1939

~

I n the spring of 1861, Tennessee joined the Confederate States of America. Most of the people in Gallatin, Tennessee—about 30 miles northeast of Nashville—were quick to rally around the Confederate "Stars and Bars." At first, eight-year-old Opie Read was not impressed. He described his reaction seventy years later in his book *I Remember*: "To me, it was not so attractive as the old flag, its stripes being too broad."

During the flag-raising ceremony, Opie's school teacher inquired, "Do you know what this means?"

Just then, a marching band began to play. The air trembled with the roll of the drum and the trill of the fife. Opie answered with one word: "Music!"

Shouting above the din, the instructor corrected him: "Thoughtless boy! It means war, death, and destruction."

Over the next five years, Opie Read would see plenty of all three.

Born in Nashville on December 22, 1852, Opie Percival Read was the eleventh child of Guilford and Elizabeth Wallace Read. Six of their children were still living when Opie arrived. The eldest, William, was more than twenty years older than his newest sibling. Next in age came Cordelia, then Guilford Jr., Martha, Harriet, and James.

Opie Percival Read circa 1889.

When Opie was a few weeks old, the Reads moved to Gallatin. In Opie's words the city of about 900 people was "the aristocratic center of a blue grass section where were produced able lawyers, doctors, preachers, but more especially race horses that achieved distinction and victory throughout the Anglo-Saxon world."

Guilford Read's machine shop and carriage-making factory stood on North Water Street in Gallatin. The Read family lived on a farm in a white, two-story house. Black locust trees edged the sidewalk in front.

In 1860 Confederate sympathies ran high in Gallatin. When Abraham Lincoln was elected president of the United States in November, he became, in Opie's words, "the protagonist of a mighty drama [that] came upon our town with the bluster of a storm." Many of Opie's neighbors could not stomach "the disgrace of a rail-splitter in the White House" and believed withdrawing from the Union was the only acceptable response; however, Guilford Read and a number of others disagreed. A group of "the hot heads," as Opie termed them, warned Read that his home might be raided if he continued to oppose secession.

"All right," Read retorted, "and you'll be met with a double-barreled shot gun loaded with scrap iron."

The Reads' house was never attacked, but Opie did become a target. Two boys waylaid him, knocked him down, and threw him into a muddy ditch. Opie told his parents he slipped and fell into the muck. That way, he could plot his revenge in secret. Although only eight years old, Opie was a large, sturdy boy. A neighbor had once called him clumsy, and Opie himself admitted that he had big feet. Nevertheless, he had become fairly good at boxing. He soon paid the bullies back for what they had done to him.

"Meeting the boys, one at a time," he wrote in *I Remember*, "I beat them senseless."

The youngster's willingness to accost his enemies did not surprise Lilah, his African-American nurse. She knew Opie well. On one occasion she overheard Mrs. Read discussing the possibility of Opie becoming a preacher. Lilah was a slave and normally did not participate in family conversations. In this case, however, she was unable to suppress her astonishment. She blurted that Opie would be miserable as a preacher. After all, she pointed out, he was always happiest when he had just had a fight with another boy!

Many years later, while talking to his close friend Maurice Elfer, Opie said of his mother: "There never was a more kindly creature. . . . She was tall . . . and strong. . . . She rarely knew what weariness was. I have known her to get out of bed in the night to deliver a sermon with which she had been inspired while asleep."

Opie described his father as "fearless, except as he was commanded to fear the Lord." Although Opie loved and respected the elder Read, he had trouble understanding his attitude toward imagination and storytelling.

"To my father a novel was a crime," Opie later told Maurice Elfer.

Guilford Read considered works of fiction to be "a pack of lies." Upon learning that *Robinson Crusoe* was not a true account but a novel written by Daniel Defoe, he ordered his daughter Harriet to throw the book into the fire. In contrast Opie was "completely enthralled" by the human imagination. He listened with delight to an elderly African-American shoemaker in Gallatin who recited tales of Bre'er Fox and Bre'er Rabbit, long before Joel Chandler Harris made the stories famous.

Opie himself was gifted at spinning yarns. He often entertained his friends with an original adventure tale he called "Robert the Good Shooter." He also frightened the slave children—and himself—with ghost stories.

"Not with a kindly eye did my father look upon it all," Opie wrote in *I Remember*. "He feared that I might become an habitual liar."

Other family members did not share Guilford Read's low opinion of literature. When Opie's cousin George Wallace saw Opie reading *David Copperfield* by Charles Dickens, he told the boy: "That book . . . will be living when thousands of libraries have perished."

In mid-April 1861 the Reads' peaceful life in the rolling hills of Middle Tennessee changed forever. Confederate forces seized Fort Sumter in South Carolina. Friends swarmed to the Read home to discuss the alarming news. Years later, Opie described the scene to Maurice Elfer: "Vividly I recall an old fellow whom I did not believe had any feeling whatever. He turned his face toward me as tears rolled down his cheeks. . . . 'Merciful Lord,' he moaned, 'the world is nearing its bloody end!'"

As Opie watched Gallatin's leaders raise the Confederate flag, he began to see that reality could be even more fascinating than fiction. He longed to taste the glory of war. He later recalled: "I couldn't grasp the meaning of it all, but I wanted to fight to music. My combats had never been set to tune, and I longed to fire a gun with Dixie stirring in my soul. My eldest brother . . . joined the cavalry, and when he had come home to spend a night with us before going to the front, I filched his saber, unsheathed the bright war blade and slept with it."

Rebel victories in Virginia and Missouri intensified Opie's desire to wage battle to music. From what he had heard, however, it seemed unlikely that he would have to defend Gallatin against the Yankees. Although the city was an important river and railroad town, the entire Middle Tennessee region was protected from invasion by a defense line anchored at Bowling Green, Kentucky. Fort Donelson on the Cumberland River and Fort Henry on the Tennessee stood ready to repulse an attack by water.

As 1861 drew to a close, Opie celebrated his ninth birthday. On January 22, 1862, Federal gunboats began shelling Fort Henry. Because of heavy winter rains, the Cumberland River was high, allowing the enemy easy access to the fort. Meanwhile, a Union victory at Fishing Creek, Kentucky, severely damaged the defensive line northeast of Bowling Green.

Fort Henry surrendered to Union general Ulysses S. Grant's forces on February 6. Fort Donelson fell ten days later. On February 18 Gallatin resident Laura Williams, age eighteen, wrote to her brother, a third sergeant with the Second Tennessee Regiment: "After our defeat at Fort Donelson everybody seems deranged. . . . We heard the [Federals] were about 40 miles from here and yesterday everybody was huddled around the streets looking every minute for them to come to Gallatin."

Opie wondered if the reports he had heard about the Yankees were true. In *I Remember* he stated: "The story had been told . . . that each man who marched in the ranks of the North wore a pair of horns not always hidden by his cap."

When the Yankees paraded into Gallatin to the beat of a brass band, Opie was there. He observed that the soldiers were "trim and neat in their blue garb . . . orderly, silent, and looking neither to the right nor to the left, but straight ahead as if their mission lay far beyond us."

Opie and his friends went to the enemy's camp to get a better look at the "Northern devils."

"Removing their head gear they revealed no horns," Opie recalled. "Nor did close search bring out a difference between them and 'our folks' except their accents which to us seemed harsh."

As the war continued, more and more troops were needed at the front. The Union garrison at Gallatin was gradually reduced. On August 12, 1862, the town was captured by Confederate general John Hunt Morgan and his band of horsemen. Morgan's raiders had already successfully attacked and raided other Union outposts in Kentucky and Tennessee. Opie had a personal interest in Morgan's exploits, for his cousin George, lover of literature, was an officer in Morgan's cavalry.

In *I Remember* Opie described the Confederate occupation as "a time of great jubilation, Morgan's men singing as they rode through the streets." On August 21 the festivities were interrupted when Union troops under General R. W. Johnson arrived to reclaim Gallatin.

Although Opie was ordered to stay in the cellar with a number of other boys, he managed to sneak out. He approached a bugler who was on horseback and asked if he could ride along with him. The soldier—half-drunken, according to Opie—agreed under one condition: Opie had to go fill his canteen with peach brandy and bring it back to him. Opie did not find the assignment difficult. He ran to the home of an African-American man he knew sold liquor. After trading his own jacket for the brandy, he returned to the bugler.

Seated on the horse's rump behind the saddle, Opie eagerly took in the sights and sounds that surrounded him: "Now with shouts and

Opie Percival Read in his later years.

songs of discordant loudness we rode forth to battle. The morning was beautiful. The iron weed was in bloom, and sitting on its purple top, the dryfly sang the song of midsummer. . . . The troop dashed out upon a bluegrass plane. Over the brow of a green slope the enemy was advancing. It was to be a cavalry fight, a shock of horse and a clash of saber."

Glancing to his right, Opie noticed Morgan's men stretched out in a long line. He looked ahead and saw the enemy in a similar form. His riding companion blew his bugle. The two lines of soldiers rushed toward each other, sabers drawn.

"It was an entrancing sight," Opie wrote years later. "Not a pistol nor a carbine had been fired. There was no dust. . . . Far to the right as the sabers gleamed there were two long lines of brightness, broken into whirling glints of sun-reflecting silver."

The nine year old found the scene beautiful, not horrible. He was in the midst of the battle, yet set apart. Every detail was sharp and clear. He noticed a martin catching a bee, saw an ironweed bending under a lark, and he watched as a terribly wounded man fell to the ground. The fighting grew more fierce. "My friend blew his bugle. The horses leaped forward. The line of blue began to grow ragged. Wilder shouts, and now gunshots with, it seemed to me, the intruding yap, yap of a stray dog. The enemy was in flight."

Opie's comrade rose up in his stirrups, waved his bugle high in the air, and blew a "triumphant blast." Settling back into the saddle, he lifted his bugle again, but this time no sound came out. Opie thought perhaps the man had taken pity on the beaten foe. When their horse bounded forward, the bugler began to lean back against the boy.

"Don't, please," Opie said. "You are about to shove me off."

The bugler leaned back even more. Opie shifted to one side, reached around, and grabbed the saddle horn. At that moment he discovered the soldier had been shot in the chest.

"I looked and saw that death had thrown its film into his eyes," Opie wrote in *I Remember*. "I stretched down and with my foot kicked the stirrup away. The bugler leaned over and fell to the ground. I got into the saddle, rode up to a fence, got down and ran back over the grassy slope."

By now Morgan's men had given chase to the retreating Federals, and the battlefield was deserted. As Opie made his way home, he could not help staring at the bodies of the fallen soldiers. Years later, he told Maurice Elfer about the sight that stopped him cold that day: "Suddenly I staggered and fell upon my knees, for there, on the ground, lay my cousin Wallace, with a smile of death upon his lips, and I knew that he had died bravely."

Opie gazed at the young man who would never again encourage him to read the masterpieces of Dickens. At last he understood his elderly neighbor's tears and his teacher's dark prophecy, shouted above the noise of the marching band.

Knowing he would have to confess his exploits to his parents, Opie decided his only hope was to thrill them with his story. When he was finished talking, his mother sat with her hands clasped. His father spoke: "I am proud of you. With your courage you have honored the family name. But I have given it out that I am to whip you and the Lord must not detect me in a lie."

Opie later reported that the lash fell upon him with gentleness, "just hard enough to keep the Lord from catching [my father] in a lie."

On August 22 Morgan issued a proclamation, congratulating his men and declaring: "The utter annihilation of General Johnson's brigade . . . raises your reputation as soldiers and strikes fear into the craven hearts of your enemies."

In spite of Morgan's confident words, Gallatin did not remain in Confederate hands much longer. Union general Eleazar Arthur Paine was placed in command of the town in November 1862. Paine was assigned to protect the rail and water lines and police the civilian population. Gallatin's residents found the general's last name to be singularly appropriate. In her diary sixteen-year-old Alice Williamson of Gallatin referred to Paine as "old Payne," "our king," "his lordship," "old hurricane," and "old Marster." Opie remembered seeing him on a street corner delivering "fatal sentences" upon people who were brought before him.

After the war Gallatin gradually adjusted to the defeat of the Confederacy. One day in 1865, Opie, by then age twelve, eavesdropped on a conversation between his father and a preacher.

"The Lord's will be done," the preacher said, referring to the war.

Guilford Read replied, "Then it was the will of God that the South should be whipped."

"Well, in a way, yes," the preacher said.

"Then the North and not the South was right."

"Brother, I can't say that."

"Which, then, Brother Wilson, is to say that the Lord was wrong."

"Merciful God, let me get out of this house of sin!" the preacher shouted and rushed out.

Opie Read never lost his love for a good story. He eventually became a journalist, newspaper editor, novelist, humorist, lecturer, and folk philosopher. As an adult, according to Maurice Elfer, Opie was a "big, tall, hazel-eyed, well-mannered, friendly man." Biographer Robert L. Morris wrote, "He had the frame and the countenance of the old frontiersmen; a great voice, a vigor of speech, and a racy flow of backwoods anecdotes." The *New York Times* described him as "a giant of a man, with a fondness for a great, down-sweeping pipe."

On June 30, 1880, Opie married Ada Benham, a native of Fort Wayne, Indiana. Like Opie she was fond of reading and music. She played the piano beautifully. The couple raised three sons, Guilford, Philo, and Leslie, and two daughters, Harriet and Elaine.

Opie Read authored more than fifty books, including *My Young Masters* (about the Civil War), *Odd Folks* (stories and character sketches about personality quirks and unusual events in the lives of ordinary people), and *The New Mr. Howerson* (about a man driven into the fold of an anarchist group in Chicago around 1910). Throughout his writing career he was openly compared with Benjamin Franklin, Joel Chandler Harris, and Mark Twain. Opie had many famous friends, among them Twain, William Jennings Bryan, Theodore Roosevelt, James Whitcomb Riley, Warren G. Harding, and Eugene Field.

Opie Percival Read died at his home in Chicago on November 2, 1939. He was nearly eighty-seven years old. On one of the last days of his life, he recited a poem for Maurice Elfer and told him a few jokes.

In the end the boy who wanted to fight to music gave the people of his native land a new song to sing when they needed it most. His experiences during the Civil War years remained in the back of his mind, and he explored them often in his writing. Reed A. Baird described Opie's legacy in an article for the *Tennessee Historical Quarterly*: "[Opie Read's] role was that of a mediator between the North and the South, whose double vision enabled him to perceive the strengths and weaknesses of both sections. . . . He helped to heal the wounded psyche of a nation torn by civil war."

LITTLE REBEL

Rose Greenhow
1854– ?

~

The year was 1862; the month was March. The war between America's northern and southern sections had been raging almost one full year. In Washington D.C. a three-story building at First and A Streets had been turned into a prison. Formerly a boardinghouse patronized by members of Congress, it now served as home to enemies of the Federal government as they awaited their fate.

In a 10-by-12-foot jail cell with barred windows lived eight-year-old "Little Rose" Greenhow. She slept on a bed of straw, her head resting on a small, dingy pillow. Although she was allowed to go down into the prison yard for brief periods, she often came back to her room crying because of the rough, rude behavior of other inmates.

No one who knew the child's family could have foreseen that she would ever be subjected to such treatment. Little Rose was the daughter of Robert Greenhow, a noted lawyer, doctor, linguist, and author. The girl's mother, Rose O'Neal Greenhow—a well-known and popular member of Washington's high society since her teens—came from a wealthy Maryland family. The Greenhows' distinguished and influential friends included James Buchanan, thirteenth president of the United States, as well as U.S. Senators John C. Calhoun of South Carolina and Jefferson Davis of Mississippi. In addition, Little Rose's cousin Addie Cutts was married to Stephen A. Douglas, a U.S. senator who ran for president against Abraham Lincoln.

Although young Rose met many of these celebrities, she never had a chance to know her own father. In the spring of 1854, while Rose was still an infant, Robert Greenhow fell down an embankment. His injuries were severe, and six weeks later he died. Left behind were his wife and four daughters: Florence, Gertrude, Leila, and baby Rose.

Mrs. Greenhow sold the large family home and bought a more modest house across from St. John's Episcopal Church. There, she continued to entertain Washington's elite. Had the country not gone to war, Little Rose most likely would have grown up privileged and pampered, blossoming into a Washington belle. Instead, at age eight, she found herself locked in jail.

Her journey to the Old Capitol Prison probably began in the winter of 1859. Lines were being drawn between North and South, and Mrs. Greenhow made no secret of her devotion to the latter. With Lincoln's election as president in November 1860, the country stood on the edge of crisis. On December 20 South Carolina voted to secede from the Union. During January and February of 1861, six more states pulled out. Although Mrs. Greenhow strongly supported secession, she wept openly as her dear friend Senator Davis gave his farewell speech to Congress.

In mid-March following a long illness, Little Rose's sister Gertrude died. Rose, now seven years old, continued daily lessons with her mother in the library of their home at 398 Sixteenth Street. On April 13 Fort Sumter surrendered to South Carolina. Four more states joined the Confederacy. Mrs. Greenhow had more visitors than ever. Even though her Southern sympathies were widely known, many of her guests were prominent Northerners.

As weeks passed, young Rose may have noticed that her mother spent a lot of time writing on scraps of paper. She would not have realized, however, that Mrs. Greenhow was writing in code. Rose also could not have known that when her mother raised and lowered window shades, she was sending messages. The child had no idea someone was watching through field glasses from Virginia, across the Potomac River.

Mrs. Greenhow had become a Confederate spy. She was ideally

suited to the task. Living two blocks from the White House, she always seemed to be in the right place at the right time—and she knew the right people.

In July Mrs. Greenhow sent vital information to Confederate general P. G. T. Beauregard's headquarters: "Order issued for McDowell to move on Manassas tonight." "McDowell" referred to Union commander Irvin McDowell, and Manassas is a town in Virginia. On Sunday, July 21, Yankees and Rebels clashed in what would become known as the First Battle of Manassas, or Bull Run. Alerted by Mrs. Greenhow, the Confederates pulled in reinforcements and defeated Union troops in this first great battle of the war.

In the North panic reigned. July 22 was declared "Black Monday," as residents of Washington received the reports of death and destruction at Bull Run. In the Greenhow home, however, gaiety prevailed. Young Rose's mother and her guests chattered happily about the victory and the inevitable "breakdown of the Yankee race." They seemed convinced the war would end soon.

Over the next few weeks, Mrs. Greenhow divided her attention between a steady stream of callers and Little Rose, the only daughter left at home. Leila was living in Utah with Florence, who had married Treadwell Moore, an officer in the Union army. Moore was not the only Yankee in the family. Little Rose's cousin, James Madison Cutts Jr., had joined a Union regiment. Every member of the Cutts family was a staunch Lincoln supporter. Although visits between Mrs. Greenhow and her Washington-area relatives were somewhat awkward, they still managed to maintain a cordial relationship.

Meanwhile, a man named Allan Pinkerton had decided that Mrs. Greenhow was being treated much too cordially. Pinkerton was head of the U.S. Secret Service, assigned by the War Department to watch the Greenhow home. By late July the detective was convinced that Rose O'Neal Greenhow was involved in more than the occasional dinner party. On August 23 he made his move.

"Mrs. Greenhow . . . was arrested on Friday," proclaimed the *New York Times* on August 26. "Various persons called at her residence and were taken in custody."

Pinkerton's total "catch" might have been larger had young Rose not risen to the occasion. According to one account her mother whispered to her to go outside and warn visitors not to come near. As the child headed for the door, one of Pinkerton's agents tried to stop her.

"Turn me loose, you Yankee!" Little Rose cried, jerking her arm free. She raced outside, climbed a tree, and began shouting, "Mother has been arrested! Mother has been arrested!"

Detectives hauled her down. Mrs. Greenhow and Little Rose were confined under "house arrest." The home was searched, and every possible clue was seized. For the next several months, the Greenhows were under constant scrutiny.

Soon more women suspected of treason were brought to 398 Sixteenth Street. One of the ladies, according to young Rose's mother, "raved from early morn till late at night, in language more vehement than delicate. . . . My chief care was to prevent my child from hearing much that was unfit for her ear."

Because of her tender age, Little Rose was given certain privileges. Occasionally she was allowed to attend church, accompanied by a guard and Lizzie Fitzgerald, a maid who often took care of her. Rose was also permitted to play outside on the pavement, although she was restricted to an area "a few feet in front of the house."

Soon, the food given to the prisoners, which had at least been edible at first, declined in quality and quantity. Little Rose often went to bed hungry. In an attempt to gain favor with the guards, one of the other prisoners reported that the girl had picked up a note for her mother near the front steps. Young Rose's permit to play outside was revoked. In her book, *My Imprisonment,* published in London in 1863, Mrs. Greenhow wrote: "The poor child was, from that time, doomed to as severe imprisonment as I endured. This was, perhaps, my hardest trial—to see my little one pining and fading under my eyes for want of food and air."

Both Little Rose and her mother suffered from ill health. The Greenhow spy network, however, seemed as robust as ever. In spite of being watched constantly, Little Rose's mother continued to pass information to the Confederacy. She stitched intelligence reports into colorful tapestries and disguised classified information as letters to "Aunt Sally" about "shoes for the children."

Winter descended on the town. Fewer and fewer people attempted to visit. On Christmas Day Little Rose's distress was somewhat relieved when her cousin Addie Douglas sent a large cake and several small gifts. In addition the child was allowed to attend parties at the homes of several friends.

Darker days soon arrived. On Saturday afternoon, January 18, 1862, as Little Rose played with her dolls in the library, guards notified Mrs. Greenhow that she and her daughter were being moved. Lizzie Fitzgerald begged to be allowed to go with young Rose, but her request was denied. The child burst into tears when they parted.

At five o'clock that evening, Little Rose and her mother arrived at the Old Capitol Prison. They were met at the entrance by Superintendent William Wood. He had been warned that Mrs. Greenhow was a force to be reckoned with. He was surprised when a sweet-faced child in crinolines marched up to him and announced: "You have got one of the hardest little rebels here that you ever saw."

Suppressing a smile, Rose's mother cautioned her: "You must be careful what you say here."

The captives were taken to a room on the second floor at the back of the prison. The chamber was sparsely furnished with a straw bed, a wooden table and chairs, and a mirror. Bars were put in the window the day after the Greenhows arrived. Eventually, Mrs. Greenhow's desk and sewing machine were brought to the cell. She was given a few books and writing materials and began to keep a diary of her experiences.

On January 25, 1862, she wrote: "Rose is subject to the same rigorous restrictions as myself. I was fearful at first that she would pine, and said, 'My little darling, you must show yourself superior to these Yankees, and not pine.' She replied quickly, 'O mamma, never fear; I hate them too much. I intend to dance and sing "Jeff Davis is coming," just to scare them!'"

In general, however, Little Rose did not feel much like dancing and singing. According to her mother a typical dinner consisted of "a bowl of beans swimming in grease, two slices of fat junk, and two slices of bread." The walls of the room "swarmed with vermin," and Mrs. Greenhow had to use candle flames to destroy the insects. Little Rose's bed was extremely hard. Her mother placed folded clothing under her, but still she cried out in the night: "Oh, mamma, the bed hurts me so much."

Mrs. Greenhow also reported that her clothes were often filled with vermin after being washed and that items were frequently stolen. Little Rose's only relief from confinement was a half-hour's exercise in the prison yard, where she and her mother picked their way through mud and groups of rowdy prisoners, "followed by soldiers and corporals with bayonet in hand."

In early March young Rose became seriously ill with the measles. Her mother asked for her family doctor. Her request was denied, and she rejected the substitute sent by the War Department, calling him "a vulgar, uneducated man." April arrived and with it warm temperatures and more problems, including an increase in the insect population.

"The health of my child troubled me greatly," Mrs. Greenhow wrote. "All her buoyancy was gone, and she would now lie for hours upon my lap."

Finally the Greenhows' physician was allowed to visit. He "found the condition of the child critical," Mrs. Greenhow recorded, "and represented to the General the necessity of her having more nutritious food, also air and exercise; and thenceforward, she was taken out very generally for a short time each day by one or other of the officers."

Conditions were still far from suitable for the little girl, yet Mrs. Greenhow was convinced she was doing the right thing. Those who received messages from her approved. The Cutts family, however, severed all ties with their secessionist kinswoman.

The war was now more than a year old. Confederate celebrations of the Manassas victory had been drowned out by the noise of Union shells fired at Pea Ridge, Arkansas, and Shiloh, Tennessee. In addition the Federals now held Port Royal, Beaufort, and all the Sea Islands of South Carolina. New Orleans had fallen to the Union, as had Fort Donelson in Tennessee and Fort Pulaski in Georgia.

At a little after five o'clock on Sunday morning, May 11, the sound of a rifle shot and a loud cry awoke the Greenhows. A prisoner had been killed trying to escape. Mrs. Greenhow wrote in her diary: "My child is so nervous from a repetition of these dreadful scenes that she starts and cries out in her sleep. Horrors like this will shatter the nerves of the strongest."

The quality of prison rations deteriorated. On May 14 Mrs. Greenhow wrote that she and Little Rose had been served a small piece of fowl so tough they could not get their teeth through it. She added, "Rose cried heartily, for she was very hungry." Fortunately, one of the officers took pity and smuggled in a more filling supper.

In later years Little Rose recalled crying herself to sleep from hunger and also the kindness of other captives: "There was a tiny closet in our room in which mother contrived to loosen a plank that she would lift up, and the prisoners of war underneath would . . . lower me into their room; they were allowed to receive fruit, etc., from the outside, and generously shared with me, also they would give mother news of the outside world."

More than four months after their arrival at the Old Capitol Prison, the Greenhows received truly good news. They were being released. On June 2, 1862, the *New York Times* reported: "Mrs. Greenhow, Miss Rose, her daughter, Mrs. Baxley and Mrs. Morris, four female traitors . . . were released and sent to Baltimore last evening, under a guard, and left in this afternoon's boat for Old Point to be sent South."

Little Rose's mother signed a statement promising that she would "not return north of the Potomac River during the present hostilities without the permission of the Secretary of War of the U.S." In Richmond Jefferson Davis visited his dear friend Mrs. Greenhow and her daughter. Davis had been elected President of the Confederacy after Mississippi withdrew from the Union. He thanked Mrs. Greenhow for her contribution to the victory at Manassas.

"But for you," he told her. "There would have been no Bull Run."

As the Greenhows settled into a new life, they occasionally attracted attention. While dining at the American Hotel with her mother, young Rose took particular notice of a man at another table. She had seen him before, in Washington. The *Richmond Daily Enquirer* printed an account of the incident on June 16: "One of McClellan's officers, disguised in a Confederate uniform was recognized . . . by a daughter of Mrs. Greenhow, and when he discovered her eyeing him very suspiciously, he cut out and disappeared."

That summer Little Rose and her mother moved into a brick house on West Franklin Street. They often took walks through the neighborhood, and Rose played with the three Davis children—Maggie, Jeff Jr., and Joe. In the fall she went to school, studying French, music, composition, and sewing. She and her mother enjoyed plays at the Richmond Theater and attended St. Peter's Roman Catholic Cathedral.

A year passed. By August 1863 life in the South had become much more difficult, not to mention dangerous. The Union blockade along the coast had made food and other products scarce. Although Confederate general Robert E. Lee had defeated Union forces at Chancellorsville, Virginia, in May, Federal troops had turned the tables in July at Gettysburg, Pennsylvania. On July 4 Vicksburg, Mississippi, had surrendered to the Union.

In an effort to protect her youngest daughter and to seek foreign aid for her beloved Southland, Rose O'Neal Greenhow decided to go to Europe. Arriving in England on September 1, mother and daughter were reunited with Little Rose's sister Florence, who had come from America to see them on neutral ground. Florence took young Rose to Paris and enrolled her in a convent school.

Mrs. Greenhow's book about her prison experience was published while she was in England. Shortly before Christmas, she traveled to Paris to see Little Rose, who seemed to be thriving at the convent school. In January 1864 Mrs. Greenhow met with Napoleon III, the Emperor of France, to plead the Confederate cause.

While the Greenhows were in Europe, Union and Confederate

troops fought a number of major battles in Tennessee and Virginia. By August 1864 Mrs. Greenhow was ready to go home. Leaving Little Rose safe in France, she sailed for Wilmington, North Carolina. Late at night on September 30, just 200 yards from North Carolina's coast, her ship crashed onto a sandbar. Mrs. Greenhow plunged beneath the waves and drowned. Her body was later recovered, and she was buried with full military honors in Wilmington on October 2.

After the war in 1871, seventeen-year-old Rose returned to America to live with Florence and Treadwell Moore in Newport, Rhode Island. She married Lieutenant William Penn Duvall, a West Point graduate. One child, a daughter named Lee, was born to the couple. The marriage did not last. According to Greenhow biographers Duvall, a strict disciplinarian, found his wife to be intolerably "flighty" and divorced her.

For a time Rose toured the country, lecturing about her adventures much like famous Confederate spy Belle Boyd. The public had an interest in women who were associated with wartime espionage. Before long, however, Rose grew tired of such performances. Forsaking her homeland, she returned to France, withdrew from public view, and devoted herself to the Catholic Church.

Not all Civil War injuries were suffered by soldiers in battle. Some of the most painful wounds were borne by children like Little Rose, "one of the hardest little Rebels" anyone ever saw.

FLASHES OF BURSTING BOMBS

Eliza Lord

1852–1885

~

"You need not fear the Union gunboats," the Confederate major assured his friend Reverend William W. Lord in May 1863. "Your home is entirely out of range from the river."

His words pleased eleven-year-old Eliza Lord—or Lida, as she was called. She did not want anything to ruin the beautiful spring day. The sky over Vicksburg, Mississippi, was robin's-egg blue, and Lida could smell roses through the open windows. Around the breakfast table sat the people most dear to her: her father and mother, sister Sarah, brother Willie, and baby sister Louisa. Lida gazed at the dainty china, delicate rolls, and steaming coffee and tried to forget that Vicksburg was under attack. At least her family was safe, she reasoned. The major had said so.

All that day, May 22, the Yankees fired shells from the river up over the cliffs into town. Sometimes the explosions sounded awfully loud to Lida, and she wondered how close the bombs had fallen. Shortly before sunset, the Lords gathered in their study. It was almost suppertime, and soon their maid, Minnie, would ring the dinner bell. A few seconds after the bell rang, Lida and her family made a terrifying discovery: Their friend the Confederate officer was wrong about the range of the Union cannons.

Many years later, in a magazine article, Lida described what happened:

> [We] were just rising to go in to supper, when the roar
> and crash came. . . . A bombshell burst in the very cen-
> ter of that pretty dining-room, blowing out the roof and
> one side, crushing the well-spread tea-table like an egg-
> shell, and making a great yawning hole in the floor, into
> which disappeared supper, china, furniture, and the safe
> containing our entire stock of butter and eggs. At first we
> were much too stunned to realize what an escape we had
> made. . . . One minute later we should have been seated
> about that table, now a mass of charred splinters at the
> bottom of that smoking gulf.

It was the first time the rectory had been hit, but not the first time
the Civil War had made its presence known in Vicksburg. Like other Confederate strongholds along the Mississippi River, Vicksburg was
a key target for the Union. By taking control of the river, the Federals would cut the Confederacy in two. Transportation of troops, food,
and supplies between its eastern and western sections would be
blocked.

Taking Vicksburg was easier said than done. The city extended almost a mile along the Mississippi River. The town's streets rose up
the hills from the waterfront, forming a succession of terraces. High
atop the bluffs, 200 feet above the river, sat the Confederate fortifications. The Union navy had paid a call on Vicksburg in May 1862,
demanding that the town surrender. Military Governor James L. Autry
had replied: "Mississippians don't know, and refuse to learn, how to
surrender to an enemy."

Back then, Reverend Lord had sent his family to a friend's plantation out in the country, about 10 miles east of town. Union gun-
ners had bombarded the town for more than a month. In the end
Confederate batteries held off the assault.

During the winter of 1862–63, the Federals made four additional
attempts to take Vicksburg, approaching by both land and water. The

Like these children pictured with the 31st Pennsylvania Infantry near Washington, D.C., Lida Lord and her siblings often mingled with soldiers.

Rebels were not the only hindrance to their effort. Disease and continual rain took their toll. Flotillas got bogged down in the swampy jungles of the Yazoo Delta north of the city. Smokestacks crashed into overhanging branches. Union sailors had to combat snakes, raccoons, and even wildcats that dropped onto their boats from above. Vicksburg held its ground, but Union general Ulysses S. Grant had no intention of giving up. Amid jeers and accusations of incompetence, he regrouped for another run at the defiant Rebel stronghold.

Now the war had come right into the Lord family's dining room. A friend of Reverend Lord's named Mr. Stiles offered the family temporary housing. It bore no resemblance to the plantation where they had sought safety a year earlier. As Lida's mother, Margaret Stockton Lord, explained in her diary: "We, through the kindness of Mr. Stiles, had a refuge in his cave."

By May 1863 cave dwelling had become a way of life in Vicksburg. People could think of no other way to protect themselves. The caves were not natural caverns, but burrows dug into the hillsides. Simple constructions in the beginning, the caves became more and more elaborate as the Union assault continued. Lida remembered Mr. Stiles's cave complex as "five short passages running parallel into the hill, connected by another crossing them at right angles, all about five feet wide, and high enough for a man to stand upright."

In memoirs published nearly fifty years later, Lida's younger brother, Willie, recalled: "The entrance galleries at either end were reserved for servants and cooking purposes, and the intervening galleries and inner central gallery were occupied as family dormitories, separated from each other by such flimsy partition of boards, screens, and hangings as could be devised. . . . In the main cave a central space was set apart as common meeting-ground."

This strange abode was home to eight families and several single people, as well as a considerable number of slaves. In Lida's words they "were packed in, white and black, like sardines in a box." At one point three wounded soldiers took shelter there. Everyone slept on planks laid on the ground or on the ground itself.

The Lord contingent consisted of Reverend Lord, who spent each day in town fulfilling his duties as rector and military chaplain; Mrs. Lord; Lida, Sarah, Willie, and Louisa; Minnie, the maid; Chloe, the cook; and Chloe's two little girls. Concerning the slaves, Minnie and Chloe, Lida declared: "These faithful women served us cheerfully during the siege and stood by us stoutly afterward."

At the tender age of three, the Lords' youngest child, Louisa, was still older than several of the cave's residents. Lida wrote: "A big store-box lined with blankets held several babies, and upon a mattress on the damp floor lay a lady accustomed to the extremest luxury, with an infant beside her only eight days old."

That first night in the cave, constant shelling kept Lida and the others awake. "Candles were forbidden," she wrote later, "and we could only see one another's faces by the lurid, lightning-like flashes of the bursting bombs."

Sometimes an explosion was especially loud and the flash of light particularly bright. When that happened, the cave's occupants huddled closer together. Women sobbed, babies cried, children fretted.

The next day Lida reported: "A bombshell struck the side of the hill, caving in one of the entrances. . . . A rush of hot smoke and a strong smell of powder filled the passages."

"Such screaming and rushing you never heard," Mrs. Lord wrote in her diary. "Mr. Merriam exclaimed, 'Great God! Out of these caves, out of these caves!'"

Willie described an equally disturbing incident. During an interval between bombardments, a three-year-old boy was playing near the cave entrance under his mother's watchful eye. When the fleet opened fire again, the woman ran to get her child. Willie wrote:

> But the child, grown accustomed to the sound of the guns, knew no fear. . . . He danced like a butterfly from point to point and laughed at his mother's vain attempts to catch and hold him, while in blissful ignorance he played tag with death. With a sudden rush the frantic mother caught him with one hand, but, screaming with delight . . . he broke away. In that very instant a shell exploded where he had stood . . . and it shattered his mother's outstretched arm and hand.

Events such as these convinced Mrs. Lord that her family was not safe in Mr. Stiles's cave. Her husband agreed. Early one morning, they traveled by carriage to the suburbs. Minnie, Chloe, and her children followed on foot. Even though they were closer to the breastworks, they hoped finally to be out of range of the mortars.

"We found ourselves in a green little valley directly behind the ridge on which the hospital stood," Lida wrote. "Here, under the protection of the yellow flag, we literally pitched our tent. Sleep was sweet that night, though our bed was a blanket on the grass."

Working tirelessly under the hot June sun, Reverend Lord, his friend the Confederate major, and several other Confederate officers created a home for the Lord family in a nearby hill. Lida was delighted.

"It was the coziest cave in all Vicksburg," she recalled later, "and the pride of our hearts."

Shaped like the letter L, the new cave ran about 40 feet under the hill. A wing opened on the front of the hill, ensuring ample ventilation. An arbor of branches arched over a pine table where the family ate when shelling permitted. Other features included an open-air kitchen, a small closet for provisions, and niches for candles, books, and flowers. Mattresses were soon procured for relatively comfortable sleeping. Most of the time the Lords slept in the tent and used the cave as a shelter.

In the evenings the rector smoked his coconut pipe. The children "made mud-pies and played with paper dolls cut from a few picture-papers and magazines." Entertainment was also provided by a group of officers camped nearby. Natives of Missouri, the men had, in Willie's words, "come South as a matter of patriotic principle, and were . . . devoted to the Cause." The soldiers spent many evenings in the cave with the Lords, singing and telling jokes. They carved silhouettes of the children's faces on the soft, clay walls.

A pony belonging to one of the lieutenants was the source of much amusement. Named Cupid, its body was fat and its legs lean and short.

"He was much more like a pug-dog than a pony," Lida wrote later. "Cupid had something of the look and all of the peculiarities of a mule. He would buck and kick outrageously, and his capers provided fun for the whole camp."

Although at times life was pleasant enough, the war was never far away. In spite of the yellow hospital flag, the little valley still received its share of hits.

"Fortunately," Willie wrote later, "a majority of these shells were of the smaller sort, with the force fairly spent before they reached us."

Lida marveled at how well-trained the little ones became. "At night, when the bombs began to fly like pigeons over our heads, they would be waked out of sound sleep, would slip on their shoes, and run, without a word, like rabbits to their burrows. In the daytime they climbed the trees, gathered papaws, and sometimes went blackberrying up the road, but . . . the first sound of cannonading sent them scampering home."

"The children bear themselves like little heroes," Mrs. Lord recorded in her diary.

One day, two huge bombshells fell in a neighboring field, about half a mile away from the Lord family's camp. The shells exploded almost simultaneously, a few feet apart, shaking the earth. Lida described the scene: "The air was filled with flying splinters, clods, fragments of iron, and branches of trees. The earth seemed fairly to belch out smoke and flame and sulphur, and the roar and shock were indescribable."

Mrs. Lord and little Louisa, now four years old, also witnessed the explosion. Although horror-stricken, Mrs. Lord tried to comfort her child: "Don't cry, my darling," she said. "God will protect us."

"But, mamma," sobbed Louisa. "I's so 'fraid God's killed, too!"

Less fearful than his younger sister, Willie became quite an expert at telling which type of shell was about to hit. Cone-shaped Parrott shells (named after their inventor) could be heard a long distance away. Rifle bullets called "minié balls" whistled by with a peculiar buzzing sound. Oddly enough, they were shaped like beehives. Willie gained some of his knowledge the hard way. On one occasion, as he stooped to pick up a bullet, a Parrott shell passed over his back so close that it scorched his jacket, so near the top of his head that it stirred his hair.

Bullets and bombs were not the only hazards faced by the campers. Swarms of mosquitoes made them miserable. Thirst and hunger were daily concerns. The vines and thickets around the cave were full of snakes. One morning Lida found a huge rattlesnake under her mattress.

The Lord children worried about their father's safety, too. Each day Reverend Lord went into the besieged city to hold services at the Episcopal church. Lida's recollection was that quite a number of people attended even though "the responses were often drowned by the rattle of musketry and the roar of bombs." By the end of the war, the church was riddled by fragments of shell and cannonballs, every window was broken, and the ivy that had covered its outer walls was torn and scorched, but, in Lida's words, "no drop of blood ever stained its sacred floor."

As the days passed, the cave dwellers grew weary of their confinement and the constant tension in the air. In mid-June 1863 Mrs. Lord wrote in her diary: "I have not been undressed now for nearly two weeks and we all live on the plainest food." On June 28 her entry read: "Still in this dreary cave. Who would have believed that we could have borne such a life for five weeks? Provisions are getting scarce—but for the kindness of Lieut. Donnellan we should have been badly off."

Plagued by fear, hunger, and boredom, the people of Vicksburg still held out hope. The newspaper—now only 6 inches wide, 18 inches long, and printed on the blank side of wallpaper—continued to promise that relief was on the way.

"The undaunted Johnston is at hand," one issue declared, referring to Confederate general Joseph E. Johnston. "We may look at any hour for his approach."

No matter how long or how hard they looked, Johnston did not appear. He did not see himself as Vicksburg's messiah. Far from it. He considered his forces much too weak to fulfill that role. In a telegram to James A. Seddon, Confederate Secretary of War, Johnston stated, "I consider saving Vicksburg hopeless."

Seddon's reply came quickly: "Your telegram grieves and alarms me. Vicksburg must not be lost without a desperate struggle. The interest and honor of the Confederacy forbid it. . . . The eyes and hopes of the whole Confederacy are upon you."

The truth was, Johnston was simply not able to meet Seddon's expectations. On July 3 Lida and her family heard that Confederate General John C. Pemberton and other officers in charge of Vicksburg's defense were to have an interview with General Ulysses S. Grant.

"What could it mean?" Mrs. Lord wondered. "A sickening dread and anxiety filled our hearts."

In spite of the difficult conditions brought about by the war, the Lords and their neighbors hated the thought of surrender. To them such a thing seemed not only unacceptable but impossible. Lida had seen soldiers going and coming on the road through the valley, and although they were "pale and wasted," they still seemed "enthusiastic and determined." For her part she was "sanguine of success" and "accustomed to hardships." She could see no reason to give up now.

The men in the trenches had a different point of view. They were living on quarter rations. Many had scurvy and other diseases. Their "dietary supplements" consisted of skinned rats and mule meat. A letter signed by "Many Soldiers" warned Pemberton that the troops were on the verge of mutiny.

"There is complaining and general dissatisfaction throughout our lines," the note read. "If you can't feed us, you had better surrender us, horrible as the idea is, than suffer this noble army to disgrace themselves by desertion. . . . Men are not going to lie here and perish."

On the morning of July 4, after a quiet night, Reverend Lord came into the cave. According to Mrs. Lord's diary, he was "pale as death" and wore a "look of agony on his face."

"Maggie, take the children home directly," he said. "The town is surrendered, and the Yankee army will enter at 10 o'clock."

As the Lord family headed back into town, they stopped to shake the hands of soldiers who were "pallid, emaciated, and grimy with dust, panting from the intense heat."

"Eyes that had fearlessly looked into the cannon's mouth fell before our heartbroken glances," Lida wrote later. "'Nothing but starvation whipped us,' muttered the poor fellows."

"The hardest trial of that bitter Fourth," she continued, "was the triumphant entrance of Grant's army, marching . . . through streets plowed by their cannon-balls and strewn with the ruins of our homes."

After meeting Grant in person, Mrs. Lord conceded, "He behaved throughout our interview as a brave soldier and gentleman should."

Before long Lida and her family departed for New Orleans aboard a steamer carrying sick and wounded Confederate soldiers. Willie described the scene at the wharf: "My father's devoted parishioners waved us a sad farewell. . . . We became refugees adrift upon the hopeless current of a losing Cause."

From New Orleans the Lords traveled to Mobile, Alabama, and then to Charleston, South Carolina. Eventually, they returned to Vicksburg, where Reverend Lord became the first pastor of the newly constructed Holy Trinity Church. The 1870 census listed Margaret and all four children—Lida, age 17; Sarah, age 16; Willie, age 14; and Louisa, age 10—as members of his household.

Lida Stockton Lord married Colin McFarquhar Reed of Washington County, Pennsylvania, on April 27, 1874, in Vicksburg. Her father performed the ceremony. Six children were born to the marriage: William, Robert, Richard, Eva, Lida, and Colin. Lida Lord Reed died in 1885.

"WE CANNOT WIN"

Anne Augusta Banister

1851–1937

&

A t nine o'clock on the morning of June 9, 1864, the church bells of Petersburg, Virginia, began to clamor for attention— and got it. Members of the homeguard and militia bolted from their houses and raced toward the courthouse.

Thirteen-year-old Anne Augusta Banister watched as the frantic, discordant clanging of the bells continued. She knew most of the men and boys dashing down the road. They were the ones who didn't qualify for the Confederate army because they were too old or too young, or performed essential services for the town. They had remained in Petersburg while their brothers, fathers, and sons went off to war—to Fredericksburg and Chancellorsville, Shiloh and Gettysburg. Now the church bells were sounding an alarm, calling those who had stayed behind.

Before long women and children began to gather in the street. Anne hurried to join them. As she approached, she caught fragments of conversation:

"Five thousand Yankees—that's what they're saying!"

"How will we hold them off? Archer's brigade doesn't even have proper weapons!"

Anne knew all about Colonel Fletcher Archer's "second class militia." Her father, William Constable Banister, was a member. The battalion consisted mostly of men between the ages of forty-five and fifty-five and of boys between sixteen and eighteen. Even though William Banister was fifty-five years old, gray-haired, and deaf, he stood ready to defend his family and town.

Archer's brigade had been issued guns left over from the War of 1812. Anne had heard that none of the muskets could hit a target more than 100 yards away. Indeed, only one in three could be depended on to fire at all. Nevertheless, in an effort to prepare for an attack, the brigade had drilled for over a month in a camp at the head of Washington Street in Petersburg.

Anne continued to listen, catching bits and pieces of several discussions.

"They're even rounding up prisoners and hospital patients to fight!"

"Aren't any of our troops nearby? Won't General Beauregard send reinforcements?"

"It had to happen. Richmond is our capital city. Everyone knows if Petersburg falls, Richmond's days are numbered."

Back in March 1861 most of Petersburg's 18,000 citizens had favored remaining in the Union. The situation changed in April of that year when the Confederate States of America took South Carolina's Fort Sumter from Federal troops by force. President Abraham Lincoln called for 75,000 men from "the several states of the Union" to "repossess the forts, places, and property which have been seized."

In response Virginia seceded, aligning forces with South Carolina, Mississippi, Florida, Alabama, Georgia, Louisiana, and Texas. Governor John Willis Ellis of North Carolina expressed his reaction to Lincoln's proclamation in no uncertain terms, calling it "the invasion of the peaceful homes of the South" and "the violent subversion of the liberties of a free people." North Carolina pulled out of the Union in May, followed by Tennessee in June.

By the spring of 1864, war had become a way of life for Americans, especially in the South. Around 3,000 wounded Confederate soldiers were being treated in military hospitals in Petersburg. The town also supplied critical support for the Confederacy in other ways. Located about 23 miles south of Richmond, it was a major transportation center. The tracks of several rail lines converged in Petersburg. The Appomattox and James Rivers offered passage by water, and roads entered the city from all directions. Petersburg's cotton mills produced tent cloth, sheets, and fabric, which were stitched into uniforms by the women of the town.

Anne thought about the hardships her family, friends, and neighbors had already endured. Food was scarce and terribly expensive. Just the other day, she had seen signs advertising flour for $200.00 a barrel, butter for $6.00 a pound, and beans for $30.00 a bushel. Tea was simply not available. To make matters worse, refugees poured into the city from areas captured by the Federals.

Life had been difficult, but at least Petersburg itself had not been attacked. Until now.

Anne knew the only protection her father and the others had was the Dimmock Line, a 10-mile-long trench system on the city's outskirts. But the Dimmock Line, built during 1862 and 1863, was in disrepair, its walls and ditches beaten down by wind and rain. In most places a man on horseback could easily ride over the line. Moreover, at least 20,000 soldiers were needed to effectively guard the fortifications. A total of about 1,200 men and boys were available on June 9, 1864.

As the morning wore on, Anne, her older sister Mollie, and their mother, Mary Caroline, waited on the front porch for news of the battle. They could hear muskets firing, men shouting, and horses screaming. It was afternoon when word finally reached them that a Yankee cavalry division called Kautz's Raiders had charged the earthworks defended by Archer's brigade.

Archer's "second class militia," which at that point numbered 125 by Colonel Archer's estimate, held their own against Kautz's 1,300 Federals as long as they could. Finally, surrounded and under fire from every direction, they were ordered to retreat. Reinforcements from General P. G. T. Beauregard arrived shortly after that, and the Yankees were driven back. Archer's brigade had bought the Confederate army just enough time to save Petersburg from capture.

Mrs. Banister and her daughters called out to passersby, asking if they knew anything about William Banister. They learned that as many as twelve men had been killed in the battle, including George B. Jones, a prominent druggist, and Godfrey Staubly, a French professor from the Petersburg Female College. Years later, in her memoirs, Anne described the moment her family's deepest fears were confirmed: "I can never forget that day . . . when my uncle, Robert Bolling, drove up in a wagon with my father's lifeless body. . . . My precious mother stood like one dazed, but in a few seconds she was kneeling by my father in such grief as I had never seen before."

On June 10 the *Petersburg Virginia Daily Express* published an account of the battle, listing the dead, wounded, and captured. Under "Killed," an entry read: "Wm. C. Banister. For many years an accountant in the Exchange Bank, and one of our best citizens. He leaves a large family."

William Banister's death was "only the beginning of the horrors we were to go through," Anne wrote later. Additional Confederate reinforcements arrived to defend Petersburg, and on June 15, 1864, Union troops assaulted the city again. It was the first clash in a siege that would last ten months.

Many of Petersburg's residents fled the city, but escape was not an option for the Banisters. In her memoirs Anne wrote: "We were unable to leave due to the fact that my brother [Norborne], fifteen years of age, was ill unto death, from exposure in camp while fighting in the defense of Petersburg."

Chelsea House, the Banister home, was in range of shells during the fighting. For safety the family moved into two large basement rooms. Day after day, they tried to nurse Norborne back to health. The shelling was constant, and none of the stores in town were open. Without proper food and medicine, Norborne's prospects were bleak.

The night of July 29, Norborne tossed and turned, suffering what Anne described as "intense agony." Around daybreak he went to sleep, but not for long. A roaring, rumbling noise filled the air; window panes shattered. Anne and Mollie clutched each other in terror. Was the world coming to an end?

Men in the trenches around Petersburg wondered the same thing, and for many of them, the world did end. Union troops had dug under the Confederate works, then loaded the tunnel with kegs of gunpowder. Early on the morning of July 30, they lit a 98-foot fuse.

W. A. Day, a Confederate soldier from North Carolina, had arrived in Petersburg earlier that month. In an article for the *Confederate Veteran*, he wrote: "Our division . . . [was] among the first to arrive at Petersburg. . . . We rested a few minutes at Blandford Cemetery, then double-quicked two miles out on the Jerusalem Plank road."

Day continued with a description of what he saw after the explosion on July 30: "The place where the battery stood was now a hole in the ground, one hundred feet long, sixty feet wide, and thirty feet deep, with the smoke rising in great clouds out of it."

Within hours Confederate troops had begun to entrench a new line in front of the Crater, as the gaping wound in the Dimmock Line came to be called. They launched a counterattack, driving the Federals back. Once again Petersburg was saved.

Huddled in the basement, Anne and her family did not know exactly what had caused the blast, but as the sounds of battle reached their ears, they feared for Anne's twenty-year-old brother, Blair, a soldier in Mahone's Brigade. They knew Blair was probably right in the middle of the fighting. To their relief he returned home late that night. His clothes were spattered with blood, but he was alive. He had fought hand-to-hand in the Crater and, in Anne's words, "hoped that never again would he be in such a battle."

During the next few weeks, Norborne continued to wage a battle against his illness, a fight he finally lost on his sixteenth birthday, August 20, 1864.

The day after Norborne was buried, an old friend paid a call on the Banisters. He had heard about Anne's father and Norborne and wanted to console the family. Although he was an extremely important, busy man, he visited Chelsea House often in the months that followed. In her memoirs Anne wrote: "He came every Sunday that there was no fighting and dined with us. He was the kindest, dearest friend to my mother and to us all and as loving to me as a father. Our

Sunday dinner was like all our other dinners—Irish potatoes, corn bread, coffee made of sweet potato and sweetened with sorghum, dried apricots also sweetened with sorghum, one slice each of bacon."

The Banisters' old family friend was none other than General Robert E. Lee, commander of the Army of Northern Virginia.

During the siege of Petersburg, Lee learned that Anne and the

General Robert E. Lee

town's other children were afraid to venture outdoors because of the shelling. He invited them to his headquarters, where they could play freely. They rode back and forth from home in an ambulance pulled by two army mules. General Lee accompanied them on his horse, Traveller. After one such excursion Anne confided to her mother: "I don't believe General Lee thinks we are going to win the war." Her mother's response was chilling: "Of course, we cannot win. We are all starving."

As fall approached, the fighting around Petersburg subsided, and many of the town's citizens returned for the winter. Anne and her friends were less afraid of playing outside. They had been taught to throw themselves on the ground when they heard a shell coming. One day, however, Anne's neighbor, Agnes, ran for a raspberry hedge to take cover. The shell arrived at the spot just ahead of her, leaving a long, deep hole. Years later, Anne wrote: "We both shrieked with laughter and amazement. What little fools we were! After this the old and young would quite often go out at night to watch the mortar shells. They were like arches of fire, and very beautiful. Very few ever fell into the town."

In October tragedy struck the Banister family again. About 30,000 Union soldiers were marched west from the Petersburg lines to advance on the Boydton Plank Road and South Side Railroad. The Confederates launched a counterattack, forcing the Federals to retreat. Anne's brother Blair was seriously wounded in his lung and right arm.

Mrs. Banister went to a hospital tent just outside town to visit him, but when she arrived, she did not see him among the thirty wounded men. Thinking a mistake had been made, she turned to go.

"Just then," Anne wrote in her memoirs, "a weak voice said, 'Mother, don't you know me?' Then she saw that this ghastly poor fellow was our handsome, gallant Blair."

Anne and her mother went to the tent each day to nurse Blair, but after three days he died from his wounds. Anne was left with fond memories of her brother's good-natured way of looking at life: "My brother . . . had always been a very merry, bright fellow and when my mother would speak to him about the future . . . he would say: 'Mother, when the Yankees come in town you will have to take some officers in the house for protection and you will find many gentlemen among them, but dear old lady, be sure and look out for a commissary and a doctor because one will feed you and after starving so long, plenty will make you need a doctor.'"

The fighting continued around Petersburg for many more months. Food and supply shortages in the South grew worse with each passing week. In March 1865 General Lee's troops were defeated in an attack on General Ulysses S. Grant's army at Fort Stedman, near Petersburg. In April the inevitable finally came to pass. Anne Banister's memoirs included a description of what she saw: "The town was full of great clouds of smoke; acrid, stinging smoke. The tobacco warehouses had all been set on fire, and we knew Richmond was being evacuated. The firing of our warehouses had been agreed upon as the signal. . . . All the morning we watched our troops go quietly by. Not one soldier in five had any shoes. Their clothes were in rags but their heads were held proudly."

After the war the Banister family put their lives back together as best they could. In 1867 Anne's cousin Mary Tabb Bolling married Robert E. Lee's son Rooney in Petersburg. When Anne walked into the wedding supper, she could barely contain her excitement—and for good reason. She was wearing her first long dress, a sign to everyone that she was now a young lady instead of a child. The identity of her escort turned a few heads as well: "I was the proudest sixteen-year-old in the whole Southland, when I went in to supper on the arm of General R. E. Lee. . . . I always felt that Gen. Lee loved me as a daughter and he was to me all greatness and loving kindness—my idol."

Lee thought very highly of Anne also. On March 10, 1868, he wrote to his daughter-in-law, Mrs. Rooney Lee, that she would have to pay attention to her brothers-in-law Robert and Romancoke until she could find someone like herself to take them in hand. "Do you think Miss Anne Banister will consent?" he wrote.

Anne did not marry one of the Lees, however. Instead, she married Archibald Campbell Pryor. They moved to Washington, D.C., where they lived until Anne's death in 1937 at the age of eighty-six.

Anne Augusta Banister Pryor is buried in Blandford Cemetery in Petersburg, next to the old Blandford Church where W. A. Day and the rest of the Forty-Ninth North Carolina rested briefly on their way to help defend the town from the Yankees. The church is now a Confederate shrine.

YOUNG IN THE GHASTLY GAME

John Sergeant Wise

1846–1913

❧

L ate on the night of October 17, 1859, members of the Virginia militia assembled at the train station in Richmond. They had been ordered by Governor Henry A. Wise to go to Harpers Ferry, about 180 miles north, to crush a rebellion. At the Richmond depot a huge crowd gathered to find out exactly what was going on and to witness the departure of the troops.

John Sergeant Wise boarded the train and sat down, his squirrel rifle between his knees. A son of Governor Wise, John had been one of the first persons to hear about the attack on Harpers Ferry. According to the telegrams a mob had seized the United States armory, arsenal, and rifle factory. Colonel Lewis Washington, the great-grand-nephew of George Washington, had been taken hostage along with other prominent individuals.

John would later find out that the raid had been organized and led by John Brown. A white man from a deeply religious family, Brown believed God had ordained him to free all slaves. He was famous for leading guerrilla attacks in the Kansas Territory and had murdered six men in cold blood. His latest plan was to establish a base in the Virginia mountains from which he would help runaway slaves and direct attacks on slaveholders.

John Sergeant Wise

As John Wise waited impatiently for his train to depart Richmond on October 17, he heard a familiar voice from an adjoining car—a voice that made him cringe. Forty years later, in his book *The End of an Era*, he recalled the words that filled him with dismay that night: "Gentlemen, has any of you seen anythin' of the Gov'ner's little boy about here? I'm lookin' for him under orders to take him home."

It was Jim, his father's butler. Horrified, John shoved his gun—nearly half again as tall as himself—under the seats and scrambled after it. In *The End of an Era*, he explained why the sound of Jim's voice was so disquieting to him: "Never was autocracy more absolute than that of a Virginia butler. Jim may have been father's slave, but I was Jim's minion, and felt it. . . . What Southern boy will ever forget the terrors of that frown. . . . What roar was ever more terrible—what grasp more icy or relentless—than those of his father's butler surprising him in the cake-box or the preserve-jar?"

John heard Jim's footsteps. He listened as Jim asked the soldiers if they had seen "the Gov'ner's little boy."

Little boy? John frowned. He would be thirteen years old in two months. In his mind he was practically an adult! Suddenly Jim's face appeared within inches of his own. The butler grinned and told him to come out. John stayed where he was. Jim grabbed the boy's leg and pulled him out from under the seat. John's hands were still clutching the long rifle.

"Well, 'fore the Lord!" Jim exclaimed. "How much gun has that boy got, anyhow?"

In John's words "The soldiers went wild with laughter." Carrying the rifle, Jim marched John ahead of him like a prisoner of war. At home the boy was taken to his stepmother's room and lectured on the folly of his actions. There he stayed until the Harpers Ferry expedition left the depot.

Most of Brown's band of twenty-one men were killed or arrested in the raid. Brown and six others were tried and hanged by the state of Virginia for treason, murder, and fomenting insurrection. A few Northern extremists saw Brown as a hero and martyr. Fearing this attitude to be widespread, many Southerners became convinced that the two regions would never be able to work out their differences peacefully.

John's father, Henry Alexander Wise, hated to see such discord in the country he had served long and well. Before becoming governor of Virginia, he had been a member of Congress and a United States Minister to Brazil. John Sergeant Wise had been born in Rio de Janeiro to his father's second wife, Sarah Sergeant.

Wise's first wife, Anne Jennings, had died in 1837. Four children survived her: Mary Elizabeth, Obadiah Jennings, Henry Alexander Jr., and Ann Jennings. In 1840 Wise married Sarah Sergeant of Philadelphia. She was the daughter of John Sergeant, a distinguished lawyer and Congressman. The children of Henry and Sarah Wise included Richard Alsop, born in 1843; Margaretta Ellen, born in 1844; and John Sergeant Wise, born on December 27, 1846. Sadly for young John and the rest of the family, Sarah Sergeant Wise died in October 1850. In 1853, when John was seven years old, his father married Mary Elizabeth Lyons.

"[My mother's death] made a profound impression," he wrote later in *The End of an Era*. "She was one of those beautiful, refined creatures for which the City of Brotherly Love is famous."

Even before the Harpers Ferry incident, John Wise was well aware of the growing tension between North and South. As a child he spent most of his time in Virginia, where he was taught that abolitionists— people who opposed slavery—were monstrous creatures. When he visited his mother's relatives in Pennsylvania, however, he got a very different message. Her family considered slavery barbaric. On one occasion John's aunt called him "her little savage." On another his grandmother's white servant referred to him as a "slave-owner." Her tone made it clear that she was not paying him a compliment.

While still very young, John struggled to sort through issues that perplexed many a mature, well-educated adult. His father's slaves seemed perfectly content. He had even asked them how they felt. They had told him that they loved their master and did not want to be free. Then, on a trip to Philadelphia, John watched the play *Uncle Tom's Cabin*, based on Harriet Beecher Stowe's book. As the drama progressed to its tragic conclusion, he became more and more upset. Years later, in *The End of an Era,* he explained: "I was too young to grasp the moral of that story, yet old enough to feel my heart rebel against things which I had never before seen laid at the door of the people I loved and among whom I lived. . . . The possibility that it all might be true revealed itself to me in a way that I little expected."

His distress intensified after he attended a slave auction.

"The horrors we witnessed came back and back again to me," he recalled as an adult. "I was very, very unhappy."

He felt somewhat better after talking to his father, brother, and uncle, who assured him that they believed slavery should be abolished, but they were concerned about how this would be done.

In 1860 Henry Wise's term as governor ended. He moved his family to an estate called Rolleston, located 5 miles from Norfolk on a branch of the Elizabeth River. In November Abraham Lincoln was elected president of the United States. John heard that there was "serious and imminent danger of civil war." His only thought was "Let it come. Who's afraid?"

On December 20, 1860, just a few days before John turned fourteen, South Carolina seceded from the United States of America. Six more southern states followed in January and February of 1861. Virginia withdrew from the Union on April 17, 1861, when President Lincoln called for troops to take Fort Sumter back from Confederate forces.

"It is impossible to describe the feelings with which I saw the stars and stripes hauled down from the custom house," John later recalled. "Across the harbor at the Gosport Navy Yard, the United States flag still floated from the garrison flagstaff, and from the ships."

Before long Confederate camps filled the woods surrounding Norfolk. In John's words, "Places . . . were lighted up with camp-fires, and resounded with the joyous laughter of the soldiers, the calls of sentinels, the stroke of the axe, or the singing of the cooks and servants. . . . This thing called war was a fascinating sport." John was afraid it would all be over before he was old enough to participate.

During the middle of the night on April 20, 1861, United States forces abandoned and blew up the Gosport Navy Yard. The next morning John stared in disbelief at the once-proud ships—the *Pennsylvania*, the *Merrimack*, and others—now in flames. The barracks, officers' quarters, and machine shops had all been destroyed. Fifteen hundred huge guns had been broken with sledge hammers. John was left wondering, "What next?"

He soon found out. Henry Wise was commissioned as a brigadier general and directed to organize a brigade in West Virginia. John's seventeen-year-old brother Richard became his father's aide-de-camp. Another brother, Obadiah Jennings Wise (called "Jennings"), joined Wise's brigade. Henry Wise Jr., by then an Episcopal minister, returned to Rolleston from Philadelphia. His sympathies lay with Virginia and the Confederacy, and his family could not safely remain in Pennsylvania.

John watched enviously as his father and two brothers departed for West Virginia. His schoolteacher enlisted in the army, and classes were suspended. He began spending as much time as possible near the cavalry camp. Day after day, he practiced shooting his rifle at targets. His "poor little mare Pocahontas" carried him at breakneck speed into countless imaginary skirmishes.

Reports of a Confederate success at the Battle of Manassas filled John with pride. He experienced a different emotion when his father's troops returned from West Virginia in December 1861. The men and their uniforms looked ragged and dirty. Their once-magnificent horses now resembled "so many bags of bones."

In early January 1862 Henry Wise was assigned to the command of Roanoke Island, North Carolina. As Jennings Wise's regiment marched through Norfolk on its way to Roanoke, he stepped out of ranks to say goodbye to John and slipped him a crisp, new Confederate bill.

John never saw his oldest brother again. Jennings was fatally wounded on February 7 during the Battle of Roanoke Island. In later years John wrote about his reaction to the news of Jennings's death: "I began to realize as never before that war is not all brilliant deeds and glory, but a gaunt, heartless wolf."

John was not satisfied to merely mourn his brother. He wanted to avenge his death, to destroy the lives of those who had killed him. He cursed the fact that at only fifteen he was considered too young for military service. The war was constantly on his mind, and he spent many hours observing the Confederate navy's activities at the Norfolk shipyards. By March 1862 the *Merrimack*—half destroyed by Federal forces when they abandoned the Gosport Navy Yard—had been rebuilt as an armored warship and given a new name: *Virginia*. Not to be outdone, the Union had built a similar craft called the *Monitor*.

On March 9 John watched from a hilltop for two hours as the ironclads battered each other. "The disparity in size between the two was remarkable," he wrote later in *The End of an Era*. "The little Monitor . . . was quicker in every way than her antagonist, and presented the appearance of a saucy kingbird pecking at a very large and very black crow."

In the end both crews simply stopped fighting because neither could gain an advantage. Norfolk fell to the Federals in May 1862. By then John and his family had relocated near Richmond. Fearful that his younger brother would run away and join the army, Richard Wise suggested sending him to the Virginia Military Institute, or VMI, in Lexington. Henry Wise approved, and the idea appealed to John, who had seen and admired the corps of cadets as a small boy. He left for VMI on September 1.

Established in 1839, VMI had been created to train soldiers to guard the arsenal at Lexington. By the 1850s the institute was offering courses in a full range of academic subjects as well as providing lessons in conduct and military tactics. Students ranged in age from sixteen to twenty-five. During the Civil War many parents viewed VMI as a safe place for their young sons to continue their education and develop self-discipline. Although the typical cadet was around seventeen, boys as young as fourteen were enrolled. VMI's Board of Visitors opposed cadet involvement in battles. Students acted only as "advisers" at first, instructing and drilling Confederate volunteers. As the war continued, however, many of them fought.

John soon grew accustomed to life at the institute. The war dragged on. More than once, the corps lost time from study to attend the burials of officers killed in battle. On the night of May 10, 1864, John and his roommates were roused from sleep by drums playing "the long roll." An officer announced that the corps was being called up to support Major General John C. Breckinridge against enemy forces advancing up the Shenandoah Valley. The cadets were ordered to appear at four o'clock in the morning with canteens, haversacks, and blankets.

Stunned silence greeted his words. Then, according to John, "as company after company broke ranks, the air was rent with wild cheering at the thought that our hour was come at last."

On May 15 nearly 250 VMI cadets—ages fifteen to twenty-five—distinguished themselves in the Battle of New Market.

"We were still young in the ghastly game, but we proved apt scholars," John commented later.

John was wounded early in the fight when a Federal shell exploded in the midst of his company. He described the experience in *The End of an Era:* "Lightnings leaped, fire flashed, the earth rocked, the sky whirled round. I stumbled, my gun pitched forward, and I fell upon my knees. Sergeant Cabell looked back at me pityingly and called out, 'Close up, men!' as he passed on. I knew no more."

The day ended with the retreat of Federal troops under General Franz Sigel. When the casualties were recorded, it was clear that the victory had cost VMI dearly. Five cadets were killed in battle; five more were mortally wounded. Forty-seven wounded youths survived, including John Sergeant Wise, who had suffered a head injury.

On June 9 the cadets were rushed back to Lexington to repulse a Union assault. They did not succeed, and on June 11, Union forces burned VMI.

John spent the summer of 1864 with his father's brigade near Petersburg, Virginia. In an effort to keep his youngest son safe, Wise arranged for him to join the newly formed reserve forces. The regiment, commanded by Colonel Robert Preston, consisted of men over forty-five and boys under eighteen. John joined the reserves on October 1. On October 2 the regiment participated in the Battle of

Saltville. "Colonel Bob," as John called his commanding officer, knew Henry Wise well.

"I don't care . . . whether you get shot or not," he told John before the battle, "but, boy, I would not be compelled to tell the general about it, if you are hurt, for all the wealth of the Indies."

The Confederate losses at Saltville were quite heavy, and "Colonel Bob" was relieved when he saw that John had emerged unharmed.

"Well, the Yankees didn't kill papa's little bouncing boy after all," he observed.

In August 1864 Atlanta, Georgia, fell to the Federals. Union general William T. Sherman's forces marched through the state during November and December, capturing Savannah on December 21. Richmond was evacuated on April 2, 1865. Jefferson Davis and his cabinet fled to Danville. By then John Wise had been in the army for about ten months. He had reached the age of eighteen and had attained the rank of lieutenant.

John knew the Southern troops were in bad shape. He did not realize, as he wrote later, that they were "literally worn out and killed out and starved out." When Davis asked for a courier to carry a message to General Robert E. Lee, Commander of the Army of Northern Virginia, John volunteered. Traveling by train and on foot and horseback, John narrowly avoided being killed by enemy fire on several occasions. On April 6 he found Lee's army trying to regroup after a resounding defeat at Saylor's Creek. John's father had participated in the battle, and John was able to talk with him as well as with Lee. According to John, Lee remarked: "A few more [Saylor's] Creeks and it will all be over—ended—just as I have expected it would end from the first."

As it turned out, Saylor's Creek was the last major engagement of the war. On April 9 Lee surrendered at Appomattox Courthouse to Union General Ulysses S. Grant.

Upon returning to civilian life, John Wise found himself transformed as if by magic from a "striking young officer" to "a mere insignificant chit." He was keenly aware of his regressed status in June 1865, when he visited his uncle in Philadelphia. Instead of eating in the dining room with the adults, he was seated with the children in the nursery.

John attended the University of Virginia, where he obtained a law degree as well as a degree in moral philosophy and political economy. In 1869 he married Evelyn Beverly Douglas of Tennessee. Shortly afterward, he formed a law partnership with his father that lasted until Henry Wise's death in 1876.

A leading political figure in Richmond in the 1880s, John ran for governor of Virginia in 1885 but was defeated. In 1888 he moved to New York, where he became an authority on electrical law, acting as counsel for the General Electric Company.

John Sergeant Wise died in Maryland at the home of his son Henry on May 12, 1913. He was survived by his wife and seven children: Hugh Douglas, Henry Alexander, John Sergeant Jr., Eva Douglas, Jennings Cropper, Margaretta, and Byrd Douglas.

On May 15, forty-nine years to the day after he fought in the Battle of New Market, John Wise was buried in Hollywood Cemetery in Richmond.

THE LIGHT IN THE WINDOW

Sallie LeConte

1850–1915

~

Fourteen-year-old Sallie LeConte woke up suddenly on the morning of January 2, 1865. Someone was screaming. It sounded like Aunt Jane's elderly slave, Nanny. Panic raced through Sallie. Every day for the past two weeks a different group of Yankee soldiers had barged into her aunt's home in Liberty County, Georgia. They had overturned and smashed furniture, stealing whatever they desired. Each time, Sallie was terrified that the men would harm her, her cousins, or Aunt Jane. So far, no one had been hurt, but she was still afraid.

Nanny stopped screaming, and Sallie heard a man's voice, a voice she was almost sure she recognized. Was it possible? She peered into the hall. Yes, it was true! The visitor was her father. Sallie burst into tears and ran to him.

Joseph LeConte had left his home in Columbia, South Carolina, on December 9. He had expected to travel through Savannah, reaching Halifax, the plantation owned by his widowed sister Jane Harden, by December 12. The Yankees, however, had burned the Savannah River bridge and still maintained a strong presence around the town. LeConte had been forced to take a much longer route, covering more than 800 miles.

By December 31 he had made it as far as the Confederate camp at Doctortown, Georgia. From there he journeyed 26 miles, climbing embankments, scrambling through brush, sloshing through swamps, and hiking over frozen ground. At times his beard became encrusted with ice.

LeConte—a geologist, chemist, and college professor—later admitted the trek he undertook "was no light one to a man of my student habits of life." Fortunately he had hunted ducks in the Georgia swamps as a boy. As an adult, he was a gymnast and a strong swimmer. The trip was a physical challenge, but not an overwhelming one. Avoiding capture by Yankees was his main concern.

At nine o'clock in the morning on January 2, he arrived at Halifax. In his journal he wrote: "The old house-servant Nanny . . . unlocked the door, looked at me a moment with a terrified air, and then, uttering a wild scream . . . dragged me upstairs . . . to the door of her mistress' room."

The next thing he knew, Sallie was in his arms.

Sarah Elizabeth LeConte—"Sallie"—was born November 11, 1850, in Cambridge, Massachusetts, while her father was attending Harvard University. She was LeConte's second child. He and his wife, Caroline Nisbet LeConte, already had one daughter, Emma Florence, who was three when Sallie was born.

At Harvard LeConte studied under renowned zoologist and geologist Louis Agassiz. A native of Switzerland, Agassiz was one of the founding fathers of scientific tradition in America. He also had a soft spot in his heart for Sallie, a toddler at the time. According to LeConte "[Sallie] was very bright . . . and spoke with remarkable distinctness. Agassiz taught her the names of all his dearest specimens. . . . He was continually playing with the child, even taking her on his back and . . . 'playing horse' all around the dining-table."

In 1859 another daughter, Josephine Eloise, was born to the LeContes. She died at the age of two. Their fourth child, Caroline Eaton, arrived in November 1863. Sallie wrote to her older sister, Emma, who was in Georgia visiting Aunt Jane: "The baby is so sweet and pretty. She has blue eyes." In another letter she commented, "I

Sallie LeConte Davis circa 1867.

can hear [Caroline] screaming as loud as she can (the bad little monkey)."

By the time baby Carrie arrived, the war between America's Northern and Southern regions had been raging for two and a half years. The Union blockade of Confederate ports was causing severe shortages in Columbia and elsewhere. Sallie wrote to Emma in December 1863: "I reckon that we will have a very poor Christmas here in Columbia, and I don't expect that you will miss much by not being here then."

In spite of the hardships LeConte and his fellow Southerners faced, he had always had faith in the Confederate cause, but by December 1864, his convictions had begun to waver. Emma was safe at home, but Sallie had gone to stay with Jane for awhile. Hearing that troops under Union general William T. Sherman were headed for Savannah, LeConte set out to rescue his daughter. Seventeen-year-old Emma recorded her concerns in a diary entry dated January 4, 1865: "What a budget of bad news this morning! Father said the Yanks made a clean sweep of everything. . . . Oh, what are my feelings when I think of Aunt Jane, Annie and Ada and poor little Sallie! And father . . . every day I tremble with the fear that I may hear he is a prisoner or killed."

She soon learned that her father had arrived safely at Halifax. While Jane, her daughters, and Sallie packed their belongings, he checked on the situation at his own nearby plantation. The overseer reported "every living thing taken or destroyed."

LeConte decided to escape with Sallie the next morning. In his journal he wrote that the only mode of transportation available was "an old broken-down Yankee horse" that "looked as if it could scarcely stand." Sallie was reluctant to go. For one thing she had never ridden a horse before. After much persuasion she consented and packed her most necessary and precious items in a carpetbag.

Breakfast on January 3 was a solemn occasion. LeConte promised to return for Jane and her daughters if at all possible. At full daylight he, Sallie, and a slave named Joshua headed down Sandy Run Road toward Walthourville. Joshua led Sallie's horse while LeConte walked.

As they traveled, they heard gunfire. To LeConte's relief the popping sounds grew fainter as the group moved along.

The next morning they passed a house belonging to a Mr. Harris. Harris ran out to stop them. It was madness for them to continue, he declared. The Yankees had camped at Walthourville the night before and were certain to come down the very road LeConte was traveling. Sallie's father appreciated the warning, but he could not turn back. The Federals already had possession of the road behind them.

"Poor Sallie!" LeConte wrote in his journal. "She looks as if she could hardly sit on the horse for terror on my account and her own."

Upon reaching Walthourville the three travelers stopped to rest in a thickly wooded area near the branch of a river. LeConte sent Joshua to find out what was going on in the area. A few minutes after the slave left, Sallie and her father heard noises nearby.

"Yankees were encamped in large numbers just on the other side of the branch," LeConte wrote, "not more than 50 yards from the spot where we lay ensconced."

Fifteen minutes later, the Federals galloped by, down the very road the LeContes had just come up. Fortunately, Sallie's horse was too worn out to react. Had he neighed a greeting at his fellow steeds, Sallie and her father would have been discovered. Sallie despaired, even though she was safe for the moment.

"Oh, that I had stayed at Aunt Jane's!" she exclaimed.

All day long, Yankee horsemen galloped up and down the road, and wagons clattered back and forth. At about four o'clock that afternoon, the traffic subsided. LeConte crept on hands and knees to the road to look at the tracks. He could tell that many of the horses and wagons had headed toward Doctorville, where he needed to go. He would have to take Sallie back to Jane's house.

Joshua confirmed LeConte's suspicions about the Federals' whereabouts and agreed that they should turn back. At nine o'clock that night, LeConte knocked on his sister's door. She was disappointed that he had not escaped but relieved that he and Sallie were all right. Exhausted, Sallie fell into bed.

On January 4 Joshua and two other slaves found LeConte a place to hide—a strip of swampy ground not far from Jane's house.

"Squad after squad of Yankees [came] to the house, but found little to take away," he observed. "Sister and the girls . . . no longer feared them, for though rough and noisy they were not insulting."

By January 7 the Yankees were gone. LeConte sent Sallie, Ada, and Annie toward Walthourville with a group of other women and children and several wagons filled with trunks. His sister had so much baggage that she elected to wait until he could return for her.

That night, Sallie and her fellow refugees stayed in an empty house in Walthourville. She helped cook bacon and hominy, and prepared bedding. Spirits were high. The women talked and laughed. Babies squalled. For the next few days, the group traveled by wagon and on foot. With the help of LeConte and others, they forded a lake using large flats propelled with poles. At one point several women and children tried to ride an overloaded wagon across a swamp. The wagon stalled. A Confederate officer carried the passengers one by one to firmer ground. The night of January 9, Sallie slept on a blanket under tree boughs.

On January 10 Sallie, her father, and their companions boarded a freight train for Thomasville. For lunch they ate boiled rice, corn bread, and roasted sweet potatoes cooked over a fire by the side of the road. In Thomasville Sallie stayed with the Merrills, old acquaintances of her parents. LeConte headed back to Halifax to get his sister and her many trunks. A little more than two weeks later, he and Jane caught up with Sallie and Ada in Macon, Georgia, at Annie's home. A train carried them to Midway. There, LeConte hired two wagons to continue the journey to Milledgeville. Along the way the group was joined by a man who gave his name as "Mr. Davis."

"The young ladies don't know what to make of him," LeConte wrote in his journal. "He attracts, yet repels. Sister thinks he is a Yankee spy. He says he is a Confederate spy. . . . That he fought the Yankees all through Georgia."

As the travelers continued toward Augusta, Davis entertained them with "bright conversation." The LeContes could learn nothing more about him, and he disappeared after the group reached Augusta.

Early on the morning of February 4, Sallie and her father began the last leg of their trip. In his journal LeConte wrote: "Sallie and myself started a little late this morning for the train for Columbia, which leaves before daylight. . . . We must walk, for there is no vehicle to be gotten. The night was pitch-dark and raining. It is impossible to avoid puddles of mud and water, for we cannot see them."

Sallie was glad to be heading home, but she was still frightened. She cried as her father dragged her along in the dark through ankle-deep mud and water. At the depot they found that Confederate troops had commandeered all the cars. Fortunately, LeConte encountered a friend who offered to take him, Jane, Sallie, and Ada to his home in Edgefield and to send them from there to Columbia by carriage.

February 7 was a gloomy day—"very cold, blowing, raining . . . trees all covered with ice." The LeContes traveled 30 miles to Columbia with sleet blowing in their faces the whole way. They arrived in the afternoon.

In her diary entry on February 9, Emma expressed her joy at seeing her father and Sallie again, although she was concerned about her father's health. She also reported that her parents had agreed to let her teach Sallie "both that she may be studying and that I may learn to teach."

Having fled Georgia to escape Sherman's troops, Sallie was dismayed to hear on February 14 that the Yankees were only a few miles from Columbia. According to Emma the city streets were "lined with panic-stricken crowds, trying to escape." All day on February 15 wagons and ambulances rattled over muddy roads in drizzling rain, delivering wounded men to South Carolina College, where the school buildings had been turned into hospitals. Joseph LeConte had taught chemistry at South Carolina College before the war, and the LeContes lived on the campus. Emma hoped their location in a "hospital zone" would protect them from attack. She grew more and more upset, however, as her mother and sister threw clothes, linens, blankets, silver, and jewelry into trunks. "Poor Sallie is very much frightened and has been crying hysterically all the morning," Emma wrote in her diary.

Severe cold continued to hold Columbia in an icy grip. The LeContes were out of wood, and Sallie and her family sat shivering, trying to start a fire with a handful of wet pine. At night Sallie shook from fear as the noise of cannon fire grew louder and more distinct with each passing hour.

The next day, the mysterious "Mr. Davis" came to the LeConte home to see Sallie's father. Emma recorded her impression in her diary: "He calls himself a Confederate spy or scout and is an oddity. I only half trust him—he evidently is not what he pretends to be." Emma also reported that Davis had assured the LeContes that they would be protected during the Yankee invasion.

Sallie's father left on February 16 to take his family's belongings to a safer location. That night, the Federals began shelling Columbia. Sallie's mother decided the family should take cover in the basement. Emma wrote: "Sallie and I went up to our rooms to bring down our things. I was standing at my bureau with my arms full when I heard a loud report. The shell whistled right over my head and exploded. I stood breathless, really expecting to see it fall in the room."

When the noise had faded, Emma went into the hall and met Sallie, coming from her room.

"O Emma," Sallie said, "this is dreadful!"

Pale and trembling, she followed her older sister downstairs. When Emma tried to leave her for a few seconds to look outside, Sallie called her back in terror. She could not bear to be alone. A huge explosion shook the house, shattering windows.

The shelling continued into the next day. News arrived that the Yankees were in town, fighting in the streets. Emma had heard that the Yankees blamed South Carolina for the war more than any other state. She was afraid they would seek revenge in a most horrific way. In her diary she wrote: "Mother is downright sick. She had been quite collected and calm . . . but now she suddenly lost all self-control and exhibited the most lively terror."

On the afternoon of February 17, Emma ran upstairs and looked out her bedroom window just in time to see the United States flag run up over the statehouse. The next night when she looked out, she saw a house burning in the distance. Soon one much closer to her own was in flames. Her fears about Yankee vengeance were coming true. She wrote: "Imagine night turned into noonday, only with a blazing, scorching glare that was horrible—a copper colored sky across which swept columns of black rolling smoke glittering with sparks and flying embers, while all around us were falling thickly showers of burning flakes. Everywhere the palpitating blaze walling the streets with solid masses of flames as far as the eye could reach—filling the air with its horrible roar."

By Sunday, February 19, calm had been restored. Emma slept soundly all night. Sallie seemed to have slept well also. "O mother," she said when she awoke. "Is it already day? I am so glad—I thought the light in the window was the reflection from a fire."

The LeConte home was not burned or invaded. Emma wrote, "I can hardly help feeling that our total exemption from insult and plunder was due in some way to the influence of the strange man who called himself Davis and promised us protection."

Unfortunately, the belongings sent with Sallie's father did not fare as well. According to Emma, "Everything was burst open—all our silver and valuables stolen—articles of clothing slashed up by bayonets and burned."

Worst of all, no one knew what had become of LeConte. In an attempt to take her mind off her missing father and her ruined city, Emma devoted her time to teaching Sallie arithmetic, Latin, spelling, natural philosophy, reading, and composition.

Food was extremely scarce. "We draw rations from the town every day—a tiny bit of rancid salt pork and a pint of meal," Emma wrote. One day "as a great treat," they had for dinner boiled rice that several of their former slaves had brought them.

Much to everyone's relief, LeConte returned safely on February 26. The war ended on April 9, 1865. Physical and emotional wounds began to heal. The LeContes never learned the true identity of the mysterious Mr. Davis, or even if Davis was his real name. Another Davis, however, would soon play a significant role in Sallie's life.

In 1869 Sallie moved to California with her parents and sister Caroline. Emma and her husband, Farish Carter Furman, remained in the South. Sallie herself was engaged to Robert Means Davis. Davis followed the LeContes to California, where he tried his hand at ranching and teaching high school. Life "out west" was not to his liking, however, and he went back to South Carolina. He and Sallie kept in touch.

Sallie eventually returned to South Carolina as well. She and Robert Davis were married on January 3, 1877, in Columbia. Davis became a professor, and Sallie found herself living in her family's old house on the campus of South Carolina College. The couple had six children: Joseph LeConte, Henry Campbell, Robert Means, Isabella Harper, Elizabeth Nisbet, and Sarah LeConte.

When Sallie's father passed away in 1901 in California, Sallie was by his side. She died on November 14, 1915, at her home in Columbia, and was buried beside her husband in Fairfield County, South Carolina.

A PERFECT SHEET
OF BULLETS

Albert Butler Blocker

1844–1923

~

A lthough sixteen-year-old Albert Blocker was one of the youngest members of the Third Texas Cavalry, he held one of the most important jobs. Late on the evening of August 9, 1861, he raised his bugle to his lips and sounded the strident notes of "boots and saddles" throughout the camp. The message was clear: Saddle and bridle your horses and prepare them to be led out.

The Third Texas was about to fight its first battle. After weeks of marching and drilling, the soldiers were ready for their assignment: a surprise attack on Federal forces garrisoned near Springfield, Missouri. The men carried squirrel rifles, old United States carbines, shotguns, and six-shooters. Some of the soldiers also toted 3-foot-long knives that were, in the words of one member of the regiment, "heavy enough to cleave the skull of a mailed knight through helmet and all."

As the men made last-minute preparations and mounted their horses, they noticed the sky seemed to be waging a war of its own.

"The lightning was flashing," Albert Blocker wrote more than forty years later in his memoirs, "and the thunder was crashing and roaring down the valley of Wilson's Creek and over the hills on which our army stood."

Albert Butler Blocker

Normally a storm would not have deterred the troops from the Lone Star State. They could tolerate the rain, and so could their horses. Unfortunately, the same could not be said for their ammunition. Gunpowder and bullets were contained in paper or linen cartridges, and few soldiers in the Third Texas Cavalry had protective boxes or pouches. To make matters worse the ammunition supply was low, and there was no quick way to get more. Ruined cartridges could not be replaced.

Soon it became obvious that the regiment would not execute its plan that night. The commanding officer ordered the men to dismount and lie on top of their weapons and ammunition to protect them from the rain. Albert settled himself on the damp ground and tried to fall asleep. He was in a very different world from the one in which he had lived just two months ago.

Born on December 9, 1844, Albert Butler Blocker was the youngest son of Mary Douglass Butler Blocker, a native of Virginia, and William Johnston Blocker, a prosperous planter from South Carolina. The Blockers lived in Marshall, Texas, about 150 miles east of Dallas. One of the largest, wealthiest towns in the state, Marshall served as headquarters for the Trans Mississippi Department of the Confederate States of America during the Civil War.

Albert's father died in 1859. In 1860 Albert—or "Allie" as he was known to his family—was in boarding school. His eldest brother, William Preston Blocker, was married and living with his wife in the family home. Another brother, Eugene, was in medical school in New Orleans.

After South Carolina seceded from the Union on December 20, 1860, Albert and another brother, Frank, decided they wanted to be ready in case war broke out. They joined a group of volunteers from Harrison County called the Texas Hunters. On February 1 Texas seceded from the Union. That spring the Texas Hunters officially presented themselves as a military unit able and willing to assist the Confederate cause.

For about a month, drilling and receiving new members occupied most of the company's time. Then, in early June, the unit responded to a call from Colonel Elkanah Brackin Greer. Greer had been commissioned to organize a regiment of cavalry for the Confederate States of America. Albert and Frank bid farewell to their mother and William, who stayed behind to manage the family's plantation and slaves. Eugene had joined a different regiment.

Sworn into service on June 13, 1861, the Texas Hunters became Company A of the Third Texas Cavalry, also known as the South Kansas–Texas Mounted Regiment. Albert was proud to serve under Colonel Greer, a native of Tennessee who had fought in the Mexican War in the 1840s. He was perhaps even prouder to be associated with the regiment's lieutenant colonel, Walter Paye Lane. Lane was famous for his heroism at the Battle of San Jacinto, a clash that secured Texas's independence from Mexico in 1836.

According to Victor M. Rose, a member of the Third Texas Cavalry, the soldiers of Greer's regiment viewed Texas as a separate entity. He wrote: "To us, Texas was the 'nation,' to her alone we owed allegiance. We were allied with the other Southern States, not indissolubly joined."

Albert became one of the regiment's buglers. His job was to translate the commanding officer's orders into notes that could be heard over a great distance, above the noise of camp or battle. Specific calls conveyed commands such as "Attention!" "Charge!" "Retreat!" and "Extinguish lights!" Sometimes buglers could tell whether a particular call came from a friend or foe and could even interpret the meaning of an enemy call. The bugle also served as the camp clock, directing each of the day's activities. Equally important, buglers built morale, marking all special occasions with a flourish.

In August 1861 the Third Texas Cavalry was ordered to Missouri to reinforce Confederate generals Ben McCulloch and Sterling Price. At the time confusion reigned in Missouri. The governor, Claiborne Fox Jackson, was pro-Southern. He intended to declare Missouri a member of the Confederacy. Unfortunately for Jackson, Union sympathizers had political control over much of the state. A convention elected to consider secession had voted to remain in the Union. On July 31 unionist Hamilton R. Gamble had been declared governor.

Jackson and his supporters repaired to Albert's hometown of Marshall, Texas, where they set up a "government in exile." Unwilling to concede, Jackson was counting on troops under McCulloch and Price to drive the Yankees out of Missouri once and for all. To do this they would have to defeat Brigadier General Nathaniel Lyon. Lyon had told Jackson that he would see everyone in the state "under the sod" before he relinquished any authority to the Confederate government.

The Third Texas arrived at Wilson's Creek, about 10 miles south of Springfield, in early August. On August 9 the regiment geared up for a surprise attack on the Federals. Instead, they wound up huddled on the ground in the rain, protecting their ammunition.

An hour before daybreak on August 10, Albert and the other buglers sounded "reveille"—the traditional wake-up call for soldiers and their horses. The men of the Third Texas were just finishing their cold breakfast and hot coffee when they heard a tremendous explosion across Wilson's Creek. The blast was followed by another. "Within seconds," Albert later recalled, "a shell came tearing and crashing through the tops of the trees, right over Company A."

Victor Rose described the reaction of one of the regiment's most colorful members, Captain S. M. Hale, commander of Company D. "Git in a straight row, here, boys!" Hale exclaimed. "This is the war you all have heard talked about! *Them's* the cannon; *them's* the muskets; that great big screeching thing is a bung-shell; and them little fellows that sing like bumble-bees, are minnie-balls!"

The buglers sounded "to horses and fall in." Soldiers scrambled to saddle up and form columns. Although the Texans moved quickly, the enemy was already way ahead of them. Lyon had marched the previous night. At daylight his troops were on a hill overlooking the camp, watching the men of the Third Texas eat their breakfast. Although he was supported by German soldiers under Major General Franz Sigel, Lyon was still outnumbered. He had decided to take advantage of the surprise factor.

Colonel Greer took several companies, including Albert's, and headed across Wilson's Creek. In his memoirs Albert described what happened: "Lyon's old regulars were pouring volley after volley at

[Price's men], and it seemed that a perfect sheet of bullets were passing over our heads. The artillery on both sides was now bellowing forth along the entire line. . . . When Company A reached the top of the hill we beheld a line of blue-coats . . . about 150 yards distant."

The Yankee officer barked, "Prepare to receive cavalry!"

Greer drew his saber, waved it toward the enemy, and ordered, "Draw your pistols, men, and charge! Remember you are Texans!"

His troops obeyed, sweeping over the Federals with a wild Texas yell. In Albert's words, "The slaughter of the enemy was terrible." As Albert's battalion was being reformed to make another attack on the enemy's flank, Union cavalry appeared on a hill several hundred yards from them and opened fire. Greer ordered the Texans to fall back into a ravine to protect themselves, but several members of the battalion were killed anyway.

In the end Confederate forces won the Battle of Wilson's Creek, also called the Battle of Springfield or the Battle of Oak Hill. Price was hit in the side but survived, commenting wryly, "If I were as slim as Lyon that fellow would have missed me entirely."

Lyon himself fared much worse. After being shot twice, he was fatally wounded in the heart while riding at the head of his column. The Rebels held Springfield until mid-February 1862, when the Union regained control.

Following the Battle of Wilson's Creek, Albert's regiment went into camp for three days, "getting some much needed rest and having our clothes washed and writing letters to the folks at home, telling them of our baptism in blood."

As winter drew near, Albert's brother William accompanied a shipment of blankets and warm clothing to the Third Texas. Unfortunately the supplies could not prevent a measles epidemic that quickly spread through the ranks. Many of the soldiers developed pneumonia and other complications. Those who were still alive and well enough to travel in early December found themselves at the mouth of Frog Bayou on the Arkansas River. There they established their winter quarters, building sheds, stables, and cabins. According to Victor Rose: "As there were no rumors of war here, the boys commenced a life of pleasure and social dissipation in the fashionable circles of Frog Bayou. Dances . . . were the order of the night; and animated jig and reel followed the lively twanging of many an Arkansaw [sic] Ole Bull's fiddle."

This vacation from battle did not last long. In mid-December Confederate Colonel Douglas Cooper called for help. Cooper headed a force of pro-Confederate Native American soldiers from the region. His immediate problem was a Creek chief named Opothleyahola, whose band of Indians were loyal to the Union.

Albert's regiment and several others were ordered to Fort Gibson in Indian Territory (now part of Oklahoma). On December 22, 1861, about 1,300 Confederates marched across the prairie toward Opothleyahola's camp. Up until that time the weather had been reasonably pleasant, but now snow glistened in the cold sunlight, causing some of the men to suffer from snow blindness.

On Christmas Day Albert and his comrades made camp "in a weird-looking country, considerably broken, with mounds rising up out of the prairie like sentinels." That night, the Texans learned more about winter than they ever wanted to know. Albert, who had just turned seventeen, later wrote: "Old Boreas seemed to throw things wide open, and turned loose on us a regular northern blizzard, with snow and icicles thrown in. . . . We had to get up and face the cutting wind, which would at times almost lift us off our feet. It was the most disagreeable Christmas night that any of us had ever experienced."

For breakfast the men had coffee, cold bread, and broiled pork. Then, though his lips were half frozen and his fingers numb, Albert managed to sound "to horse" on his bugle. The men headed for the enemy camp. Soon the Confederates were close enough to see Opothleyahola's warriors, who were, as Albert put it, "massed upon a ridge of hills which seemed to rise up from the prairie."

Walter Lane later admitted, "When I looked upon that hill, crowned with Indians, I felt as if I was being ordered to a sudden and speedy death, and no benefit of clergy in the case." From time to time the warriors shot their guns or yelled. It seemed to Albert that they were taunting the Confederate soldiers, daring them to attack. Albert and the other buglers sounded the command "Charge!" It was easier said than done, as Albert later explained: "[The hills] were so steep and broken that it was impossible to ride up them. We were ordered to dismount, hitch our horses and take the hill afoot, which we proceeded to do in quick-time."

Opothleyahola's troops fired down on the Texans, wounding many of them. In the end, however, Albert proudly reported that Opothleyahola's 1,700 soldiers were "scattered to the four winds in less than a half-hour after we began the charge."

Back at Frog Bayou, the soldiers finished building their cabins and bunks. Several Harrison County men, including Albert's physician brother, Eugene, joined the Third Texas during this time. The regiments remained in winter quarters until February 1862, when they were ordered to Fayetteville, Arkansas, to repulse Union general John C. Frémont's forces.

Albert participated in battles at Fayetteville and Elk Horn Tavern, also in Arkansas. He traveled with his regiment to Corinth, Mississippi, but the day they arrived he was stricken with typhoid fever. He was not the only one. Victor Rose called Corinth "that disease-infected point."

For a week Albert lay on a pallet in his tent, only half-conscious. He was burning with fever and thirst, and in his words, "dreaming when asleep of mother and home, and of the springs of cold water" he had seen and drunk from in the mountains of Arkansas.

Albert and others who had fallen ill were transported to Columbus, Mississippi. Albert's brother Eugene accompanied them to set up a hospital. Eugene was able to place his brother in a private home belonging to a Colonel Cozart. When Albert finally regained consciousness, the first person he saw was French, a slave of the Blocker family sent to attend to him.

Under the care of Eugene, French, and the Cozarts, Albert gradually improved. By spring he was able to sit in a rocking chair and enjoy "the soft, balmy spring air" through a window. During his convalescence at the Cozart home, he received news of his brother Frank's death from pneumonia.

"Thus ended the life of a brilliant mind, a patriotic soldier, a loving brother and comrade," Albert wrote.

Finally Albert was pronounced well enough to return to his regiment, which was in camp near Tupelo. His messmates gave him "the glad hand of welcome." They had feared his illness was fatal, as it had been for so many others. Two thirds of all Civil War casualties were caused by disease rather than battlefield injuries or deaths.

In June 1862 the Confederate army ordered the reorganization of all the regiments whose terms of service were about to expire. Under the recently established conscription law, only men between the ages of eighteen and thirty-five were required to enlist. At seventeen Albert was suddenly too young to be a soldier. He was discharged.

Albert and several others from his regiment left Tupelo on June 15. Their luggage was "reduced to a change of underclothes," Albert reported, "for we gave all that we had except this to the boys in our messes."

Their journey home included travel by train, wagon, a one-horse hack, boat, a "three-seated carry-all" pulled by "a good pair of mules," a "fine and neatly upholstered carriage driven by a pair of large, high-stepping horses," and their own tired feet.

In Shreveport, Louisiana, they "found a man who had a two-horse wagon and a pair of little Mexican mules, who agreed to send us out to Jonesville, Texas . . . for $5 each." The travelers arose early the next morning but were delayed because the man had trouble catching his mules. After what seemed like an eternity, the wagon was ready. Then the fun began. Albert wrote: "Our mules . . . made a bound and began bucking, nearly throwing us out of the wagon. . . . The rattling of the wagon, as we flew along Texas Street, and our yelling and whooping brought out all the inhabitants on both sides."

The mules wore themselves out and finally "just crept along the last 4 or 5 miles, with the empty wagon, for we had taken it afoot and got into Greenwood ahead of the wagon." After giving the mules a rest, Albert and company continued to Jonesville. There, Albert borrowed a horse to complete his journey. When he saw the road leading to his home, he raised up in his stirrups, pulled off his cap, and "gave the warwhoop or Rebel yell, several times."

At the house he threw his bridle reins over the hitching post and jumped onto the front steps. A dog dashed at him, "barking like a fury." Albert recognized it as a puppy he had raised, but when it leaped for his throat, he had to fight it off with the butt of his six-shooter.

"Hello, who is that down there?" called William.

"You had better come and see," Albert replied, "or I might have to kill your dog."

"Is that Allie?" William shouted back.

"Yes, what's left of him."

William rushed down, threw open the door, and grabbed Albert's hand. "Ma, here is Allie!" he called.

In Albert's words: "Out stepped our mother from her room into the hall and was clasped in the arms of her soldier boy. 'Home again,' he said."

After Albert turned eighteen, he served a second term in the military. On April 7, 1868, he married Eliza Jane Webster, the daughter of Julia Maria Mead Steel and John Brown Webster. The Blockers had ten children: William Webster, Eugenie Burrus, Albert Butler, Louis Edwin, Eliza Miriam, Mary Steele, Charles Preston, Frank Harwood, Douglas Vaughn, and Westwood Wallace.

Albert Butler Blocker, bugler for the Third Texas Cavalry, dictated his memoirs in 1903 at the age of sixty. He died on June 19, 1923, in Shreveport, Louisiana. He is buried in the Mimosa Hall Cemetery about 14 miles northeast of Marshall, Texas.

WANT OF LEADERSHIP

William H. S. Burgwyn
1845–1913

❧

As the members of the Thirty-fifth Regiment, North Carolina Troops, set up camp in Madison County, Virginia, they could not help wondering what Mother Nature would do next. A light snow had fallen two weeks ago, in early November. Patches of white could still be seen on the slopes of the Blue Ridge Mountains. Since then, conditions in the foothills had ranged from cold and snowy to warm and fair.

The year 1862 was about to enter its final month. The war between America's northern and southern states was going into its eighteenth—and far from final—month. Leaders on both sides had come to the unpleasant realization that the dispute was going to cost more in lives, money, and time than they had imagined when the first shots were fired.

Back in the spring of 1862, the Confederacy had been forced to face the fact that one-year enlistments were about to run out for many of its recruits. Even if most of the soldiers reenlisted, they would still be vastly outnumbered by Union forces. Something had to be done. On April 16 the Confederate Congress passed a law calling for all healthy white men between the ages of eighteen and thirty-five to sign up for a three-year term of service. Soldiers in that age range who had already signed up for one year were required to extend their terms to three years.

On November 17, 1862, in camp near Madison Court House, Virginia, the First Lieutenant of Company H, Thirty-fifth North Carolina Infantry, wrote in his diary: "Discharged four men from the company; two for being over forty years old and two for being only sixteen years of age when enlisted."

His actions were not unusual. Officers throughout the Confederacy had been signing similar discharge papers for months. What was a bit unusual was that the First Lieutenant of Company H—William Hyslop Sumner Burgwyn—was only seventeen years old. He had enlisted at age fifteen.

William—called "Will" or "Sumner" by his family—was the son of Henry King Burgwyn and Anna Greenough Burgwyn. He was born on July 23, 1845, in Jamaica Plain, Massachusetts. His twin, John Collinson Burgwyn, survived only a year after birth. At the time of Will's birth, the Burgwyns had a five-year-old daughter, Maria Greenough Burgwyn, and a three-year-old son, Henry King Burgwyn Jr. ("Harry"). After Will three more sons were born: George Pollok, John Alveston, and Collinson Pierrepont Edwards.

Both of Will's parents came from prestigious families. Henry Burgwyn's grandfather, John Burgwyn, had established himself as a planter and merchant in North Carolina in 1750. Anna Greenough was the daughter of David Stoddard Greenough, a prominent Boston attorney and real-estate developer. Greenough died in 1830, and in 1836 Anna's mother married General William Hyslop Sumner, the son of three-time Massachusetts governor Increase Sumner.

Henry Burgwyn attended the United States Military Academy at West Point, New York. When he met Anna Greenough, he was involved in railroad construction in Massachusetts and Rhode Island. The couple were married in 1838. They would have been content to live in the North, but in 1839, Burgwyn inherited a fortune in land and more than one hundred slaves from a bachelor uncle. The Burgwyns moved to a home they called Hillside, located on a 4,000-acre plantation in North Carolina, along the Roanoke River.

Henry and Anna Burgwyn were not prepared for their new roles. Burgwyn had no experience in running a farm or managing slaves.

William H. S. Burgwyn

His wife felt like a foreigner much of the time: Her Unitarian beliefs were considered worse than heresy by many Southerners; in addition, she could not bring herself to embrace the idea of slavery. In a letter to her mother dated February 4, 1839, she declared, "If I were not in Carolina I think I would be an open abolitionist." About a month later she wrote, "I grow more opposed to slavery every day."

In 1849 Hillside burned, and the Burgwyns built a new residence called Thornbury. Like most homes along the Roanoke, Thornbury was a well-built, attractive frame house equipped with every modern convenience. Although days spent on the Burgwyn plantation were pleasant enough, Thornbury was a working plantation, with emphasis on "work."

During his earliest years Will Burgwyn was instructed by private tutors. At the age of nine, he was sent away to school in New Jersey and, later, Maryland. He also attended Horner's School in Oxford, North Carolina, and Georgetown College in the District of Columbia. In August, 1860, he became a student at the University of North Carolina at Chapel Hill. In 1861 he enrolled as a cadet at the Hillsboro (North Carolina) Military Academy.

With the outbreak of war in April 1861, Will enlisted in the North Carolina Troops. Because of his brief training at Hillsboro Military Academy, the fifteen-year-old was appointed second lieutenant. Will's brother Harry, just nineteen years old, was a cadet at Virginia Military Institute when hostilities began. In August he was elected lieutenant colonel of the Twenty-sixth Regiment, North Carolina Troops. The boys' father became an aide to Governor John Willis Ellis.

North Carolina was the next-to-last state to join the Confederacy, seceding from the Union on May 20, 1861. That summer, the state received several serious blows. One of these was the death of Governor Ellis. His replacement, Henry T. Clark, had to hit the ground running during a time of crisis, with little or no opportunity to adjust to his new responsibilities. Then, on August 29, Forts Clark and Hattaras surrendered to the Federals, thereby opening access to Hattaras inlet. The defenses of New Bern, North Carolina, were suddenly in danger of direct naval attack. The state raised battalion after battalion, but many of its troops were sent to Virginia to protect Richmond instead of being used to defend the Carolina coast.

Initially Will Burgwyn served as a drill master and adjutant, an officer responsible for communicating orders from the commander of his unit to the next-smaller unit. Like many soldiers from plantation families, Will was accompanied by a slave who served as his body servant. He described his body servant, Pompey, as a "valet de chambres and man of all work and deeds." Body servants typically did not follow their masters into battle but remained safely in the rear.

Although Will had been tended by slaves from his birth, he was not in favor of continuing the institution. In a letter to his father, he wrote: "I can't but think that slavery has received its death blow in this war. . . . The practice of selling captives into slavery was but the barbarous practice of an unenlightened and uncivilized people."

The Thirty-fifth North Carolina, under Colonel James Sinclair, first saw action on March 14, 1862, at New Bern. Positioned to the left of a militia group (civilians formed into military units), it did not make a very good showing. Confederate Brigadier General Lawrence O'Brien Branch summed up the situation in his official report: "The whole Militia . . . abandoned their positions. Colonel Sinclair's regiment very quickly followed their example, retreating in the utmost disorder."

Harry Burgwyn's regiment was also part of Branch's brigade, but Harry's experience at New Bern was different from Will's. In a letter to his mother dated March 17, Harry wrote: "My command was the last to leave & though I say it myself retreated in better order than any other."

Union troops won the Battle of New Bern. Nearly forty years later, in *Histories of the Several Regiments and Battalions from North Carolina in the Great War 1861–65*, William Burgwyn stated that "want of leadership" was the cause of his regiment's embarrassing behavior. He noted that the soldiers needed a "cool, brave, experienced and resourceful man at their head." The other members of the Thirty-fifth North Carolina apparently agreed. During the reorganization of the Confederate army in April, they unanimously elected Matt W. Ransom to replace Sinclair as their colonel.

Will was pleased with this change in leadership. He described Ransom as an "accomplished man and gallant soldier." In *Histories of the Several Regiments,* he proudly pointed out that under Ransom, the

Thirty-fifth "never failed to act in such a manner as to deserve and win the encomiums of its commanding officers."

That same spring, both Will and Harry's regiments were transferred to Ransom's Brigade, commanded by Brigadier General Robert Ransom Jr., Matt Ransom's brother. Ransom's Brigade was ordered to Virginia in June 1862. On July 1 it participated in an assault on Malvern Hill, near Richmond. The charge was heroic and prevented the Federals from entering the gates of Richmond. The cost in Confederate lives, however, was staggering. Will was proud of his regiment's conduct. "[The Thirty-fifth North Carolina] then and there established its reputation for unsurpassed fortitude and intrepidity in battle," he wrote in *Histories of the Several Regiments*.

When Harry Burgwyn was elected colonel of the Twenty-sixth North Carolina in August 1862, Brigadier General Robert Ransom disapproved. He considered Harry too young for the position and reportedly declared that he wanted no "boy colonels" in his brigade. In response the men of the Twenty-sixth petitioned for removal to another brigade. Their request was granted, and they were transferred, along with their "boy colonel," to the command of Brigadier General James Johnston Pettigrew.

Before the Burgwyn brothers parted, Harry gave Will—by then First Lieutenant of Company H—a parting meal, supplies, and food. In a letter to his mother dated August 27, Harry wrote: "[Will] was provided with canteens, haversack, something in it, & a good dinner in his [stomach]. Thus armed & accoutered, & with a stout heart & trust in Providence, I believe he will succeed."

His words were prophetic. On September 16, 1862, Ransom's Brigade crossed into Maryland to support General Robert E. Lee's invasion of that state. In the early hours of September 17, Will took his place with the Thirty-fifth North Carolina at Sharpsburg, along Antietam Creek. Lee's forces were badly outnumbered by those of Union general George B. McClellan. Not only that, thousands of Confederates were unable to participate in the fighting because they had no shoes. After the battle the *Richmond Daily Dispatch* commented: "We cease to wonder at the number of stragglers, when we hear how many among them were shoeless, with stone bruises on their feet."

In a letter to Harry dated September 23, Will described his experience under fire:

> The brigade was formed in line of battle and marched splendidly through a severe shower of grape, cannister, and shell but not a man wavered till we came to a fence right in front . . . and just then the shells and things came thick and fast and at this very time my second lieutenant was shot. . . . I jumped in front of the regiment and tried all I could do to form the regiment . . . and then General Ransom gave the command "Forward." The men hesitated a little and I seized the colors from the color bearer and called on the men to follow.

Will's regiment charged through a line of woods, then had to fall back and hit the ground to avoid being destroyed by a Yankee battery.

"We were in a little hollow," he wrote Harry, "and the grape and cannister passed about three or four feet above us. . . . We were shelled there all day till about 5:00."

In *Histories of the Several Regiments*, Will told of an incident at Antietam involving a soldier named Walter Clark of the Thirty-fifth North Carolina. "Little Clark," as he was called by the regiment, had also been a cadet at Hillsboro when the war broke out. He was even younger than Will, just fourteen when he joined the army.

"When going into the fight that morning," Will wrote, "the field officers had all dismounted except Little Clark, who persistently sat in his saddle when a big mountain private, I think from Company B, ran forward and pulled [Clark] from his horse, exclaiming, 'Git off'n this horse, you darned little fool, you'll git killed.'"

At that point a minié ball struck Clark's hand, leaving a mark that could still be seen many years later, after Clark became a well-known lawyer, editor, and author.

The Battle of Antietam (also called Sharpsburg) became known as the bloodiest day of the war. Casualties were enormous on both sides. The victory went to the North, but Lee escaped across the Potomac into Virginia. Colonel Ransom praised Will for his actions, and brother Harry expressed his pride in a letter to his parents: "I was perfectly certain he would behave well," he wrote, "but it is most gratifying to hear that he extorted an encomium from Ransom himself."

The experience at Antietam left Will feeling like a seasoned veteran despite his youth. In a letter to his father, he wrote, "My beard has grown astonishingly, being now more than an inch in length and I imagine a person would take me to be much older than I am and I am presumptive enough to think I am competent to fill the majority of a regiment which I would like to get."

The Burgwyns' delight with Will's gallantry at Antietam was tempered by other news. Will and Harry's cousin George Burgwyn Anderson was fatally wounded in the battle and died soon afterward. His was the first battle death in the Burgwyn family. Before long the war would claim the life of one even dearer to Henry and Anna Burgwyn.

By December 1862 all soldiers deemed too young or too old under the new conscription law had been discharged from the Thirty-fifth North Carolina. Seventeen-year-old Will somehow managed to exempt himself. As a result on Saturday, December 13, he found himself defending a position on Marye's Heights, overlooking the town of Fredericksburg, Virginia.

"At 5:00 a.m. we were formed into line ready to take our position in the line of battle," he wrote in his diary. "From 11:00 a.m. until dark there was an incessant roar of small arms and artillery and the enemy's loss is dreadful."

The Battle of Fredericksburg went to the Confederates. They lost 1,200 men in the attack. The Federals lost 7,000. On December 17 in a letter to his father, Will wrote: "The battle is over. No more the enemy's cannon thunders forth its terrible missiles of death and the roar of musketry is for the time silenced and nothing now remains but the dreadful spectacle of the terrible combat and God in His merciful providence has preserved me unhurt and untouched through the five days and nights and a half of the dreadful carnage."

July found the Thirty-fifth North Carolina on fatigue duty, strengthening entrenchments at Bottom's Bridge, Virginia. In his diary on July 1, Will described a routine day of physical labor. He had no idea that even as he wrote the entry, Harry lay dead on the battlefield at Gettysburg, Pennsylvania. On July 12 Will finally heard that his brother had been killed. At first he was skeptical and wrote in his diary, "I could not bear to believe it and do not."

On July 13 during a visit to Petersburg, Will was told the story of Harry's death was "certainly incorrect." He telegraphed the good news to his mother. On July 14, however, he learned the truth: Harry really was gone.

"I can hardly bear the thought of losing him and have no one to console with me," his diary entry declared. "I am indeed wretched."

In 1863 Will's regiment saw action in eastern North Carolina. He also fought in the Battle of Drewry's Bluff, Virginia, in May 1864. By then he had been transferred at his request to the staff of Brigadier General Thomas L. Clingman, a close friend of his father.

On June 1, 1864, in battle at Cold Harbor, Virginia, Will received "a tremendous blow . . . about the knee making me fall like an ox and suffering intense pain." Soldiers carried him on a stretcher to the brigade hospital, where surgeons "put me under the influence of chloroform and probed and dressed my wound which they told me had struck about one-half inch below the right knee."

By July 21 Will had recovered enough to rejoin Clingman at Petersburg. On September 30 he was captured by the Federals, and he spent the next eight months in prison at Fort Delaware. While there, on Christmas Eve 1864, he received shocking news: "Heard from some officers lately arrived that I had been published in the papers as dead and my obituary written," he wrote in his diary.

Will immediately alerted his mother in a letter, asking if she had been under the impression that he was dead or had seen any such report. Paroled in late February of 1865, Will was surrendered on April 26 with General Joseph E. Johnston's army at the Bennett House near Durham Station, North Carolina. General Lee's troops had surrendered at Appomattox on April 9. The war was over.

Will picked up his life and moved on. After graduating from the University of North Carolina, he completed law studies at Harvard. He began practicing law in Baltimore in 1869. In 1874 he enrolled in Washington Medical University, receiving his M.D. two years later. He never applied for a license to practice medicine.

In November 1876 Will married Margaret Carlisle Dunlop of Richmond, Virginia. The couple left Maryland for Henderson, North Carolina, in 1882. There Will founded the Banking House of W.H.S. Burgwyn and established a tobacco factory. Although his foray into the tobacco business failed, his banking career flourished. He also served as a colonel in the United States army during the Spanish-American War. He and Margaret had no children.

William Hyslop Sumner Burgwyn died on January 3, 1913, at the age of sixty-seven. He is buried in Raleigh. His older brother Harry achieved fame as the "boy colonel," but Will also demonstrated leadership ability and courage beyond his years. In the words of Brigadier General Thomas Clingman, "He . . . always showed himself intelligent, energetic, and efficient. . . . He carried out orders with the same alacrity in danger that he did out of it."

BIBLIOGRAPHY

General References

McPherson, James M. *Battle Cry of Freedom: The Civil War Era*. New York: Ballantine Books, 1988.

Marten, James. *The Children's Civil War*. Chapel Hill: The University of North Carolina Press, 1998.

Varhola, Michael J. *Everyday Life during the Civil War*. Cincinnati, Ohio: Writer's Digest Books, 1999.

Volo, Dorothy Denneen, and James M. Volo. *Daily Life in Civil War America*. Westport, Conn.: Greenwood Press, 1998.

War of the Rebellion Official Records of the Union and Confederate Armies. Online: www.ehistory.com/uscw/library/or/index.cfm.

Werner, Emmy E. *Reluctant Witnesses: Children's Voices from the Civil War*. Boulder, Colo.: Westview Press, 1998.

Wiley, Bell Irvin. *The Life of Billy Yank*. 1952. Reprint, Baton Rouge: Louisiana State University Press, 1978.

———. *The Life of Johnny Reb*. 1943. Reprint, Baton Rouge: Louisiana State University Press, 1978.

Anne Augusta Banister

Banister, Anne A. "Incidents in the Life of a Civil War Child." Harrison Henry Cocke Papers, Southern Historical Collection, University of North Carolina, Chapel Hill.

Lee, Robert Edward. *Recollections and Letters of General Robert E. Lee by his son, Captain Robert E. Lee*. Garden City, N.Y.: Garden City Publishing Co., 1924.

Robertson, William Glenn. *The Petersburg Campaign: The Battle of Old Men and Young Boys, June 9, 1864*. Lynchburg, Va.: H. E. Howard, 1989.

Ryan, James H. *The Battle of the 9th of June, 1864*. Petersburg, Va.: Historic Petersburg Foundation, 2000.

Albert Butler Blocker

Barron, S. B. *The Lone Star Defenders: A Chronicle of the Third Texas Cavalry, Ross' Brigade*. New York: The Neale Publishing Company, 1908.

Bearss, Edwin C. *The Battle of Wilson's Creek*. Springfield, Mo.: Wilson's Creek National Battlefield Foundation, 1985.

————. "The Civil War Comes to Indian Territory, 1861, The Flight of Opothleyoholo." *Journal of the West* 11 (1972): 9–42.

Lale, Max S. "The Boy-Bugler of the Third Texas Cavalry: The A. B. Blocker Narrative." *Military History of Texas and the Southwest*, 1978–79.

Lane, Walter Paye. *The adventures and recollections of Sir Walter P. Lane*. Marshall, Tex.: News Messenger Publishing Co., ca. 1928.

Rose, Victor M. *Ross' Texas Brigade*. Louisville, Ky.: The Courier-Journal Company, 1881.

William H. S. Burgwyn

Davis, Archie K. *Boy Colonel of the Confederacy: The Life and Times of Henry King Burgwyn, Jr*. Chapel Hill: University of North Carolina Press. 1985.

Schiller, Herbert M., ed. *A Captain's War: The Letters and Diaries of William H. S. Burgwyn*. Shippensburg, Pa.: White Mane Publishing Company, Inc. 1994.

Maggie Campbell

Deland, Margaret. *If This Be I As I Suppose It Be*. New York: D. Appleton-Century Company, Inc., 1936.

McCarthy, Bill. "One Month in the Summer of '63: Pittsburgh Prepares for the Civil War," (Part I). *Pittsburgh History* 81, no. 3 (Fall 1998): 118–133.

———. "One Month in the Summer of '63: Pittsburgh Prepares for the Civil War," (Part II). *Pittsburgh History* 81, no. 4, (Winter 1998/99): 156–69.

Reep, Diana C. *Margaret Deland*. Boston: Twayne Publishers, 1985.

Thomas, Edison H. *John Hunt Morgan and His Raiders*. Lexington: University Press of Kentucky, 1985.

John Henry Crowder

Glatthaar, Joseph T. "The Civil War through the Eyes of a Sixteen-Year-Old Black Officer: The Letters of Lieutenant John H. Crowder of the 1st Louisiana Native Guards." *Louisiana History* 35, no. 2 (Spring 1994): 201–16.

Hollandsworth, James G., Jr. *The Louisiana Native Guards: The Black Military Experience during the Civil War*. Baton Rouge: Louisiana State University Press, 1995.

Joshi, Manoj K., and Joseph P. Reidy. "'To Come Forward and Aid in Putting Down This Unholy Rebellion': The Officers of Louisiana's Free Black Native Guard during the Civil War Era." *Southern Studies* 21, no. 3 (Fall 1982): 326–42.

Trudeau, Noah Andre. *Like Men of War: Black Troops in the Civil War, 1862–1865*. New York: Little, Brown and Company, 1998.

Westwood, Howard C. "Benjamin Butler's Enlistment of Black Troops in New Orleans in 1862." *Louisiana History* 1 (Winter 1985).

Edwin Fitzgerald (Foy)

Bernstein, Iver. *The New York City Draft Riots*. New York: Oxford University Press, 1990.

Fields, Armond. *Eddie Foy: A Biography of the Early Popular Stage Comedian*. Jefferson, N.C.: McFarland & Company, Inc., 1999.

Foy, Eddie, and Alvin F. Harlow. *Clowning Through Life*. New York: E.P. Dutton & Co., 1928.

Jesse Root Grant

Grant, Jesse. *In the Days of My Father General Grant.* New York: Harper & Brothers Publishers, 1925.

Grant, Julia Dent. *The Personal Memoirs of Julia Dent Grant.* New York: G. P. Putnam's Sons, 1975.

Grant, Ulysses S. *Personal Memoirs. 1885–86.* New York: Bartleby.com, 2000. Online: www.bartleby.com/1011/.

Rose Greenhow

Beymer, William Gilmore. "Mrs. Greenhow, Confederate Spy," in *The Women's War in the South,* edited by Charles G. Waugh and Martin H. Greenberg, 31–51. Nashville, Tenn.: Cumberland House, 1999.

Burger, Nash K. *Confederate Spy: Rose O'Neale Greenhow.* New York: Franklin Watts, Inc., 1967.

Greenhow, Rose O'Neal. *My Imprisonment and the First Year of Abolition Rule at Washington.* London: Spottiswoode and Co., 1863.

Ross, Ishbel. *Rebel Rose.* New York: Harper & Brothers Publishers, 1954.

Susie Baker King

Berlin, Ira, Joseph P. Reidy, and Leslie Howard, eds. *The Black Military Experience.* New York: Cambridge University Press, 1982.

Johnson, Whittington B. *Black Savannah 1788–1864.* Fayetteville: University of Arkansas Press, 1996.

Johnson, Whittington B. "Free African-American Women in Savannah, 1800–1860: Affluence and Autonomy Amid Adversity." *Georgia Historical Quarterly* 76, no. 2, (Summer 1992): 260–83.

Looby, Christopher, ed. *Complete Civil War Journal and Selected Letters of Thomas Wentworth Higginson*. Chicago: The University of Chicago Press, 2000.

Romero, Patricia W., ed. *A Black Woman's Civil War Memoirs*. New York: Markus Wiener Publishing, 1988.

Sallie LeConte

Jones, Katharine M. *Heroines of Dixie: Confederate Women Tell Their Story of the War*. Indianapolis: Bobbs-Merrill, 1955.

LeConte, Emma. *When the World Ended*. Edited by Earl Schenck Miers. New York: Oxford University Press, 1957.

LeConte, Joseph. *The Autobiography of Joseph LeConte*: Electronic Edition. Documenting the American South, University of North Carolina at Chapel Hill Libraries. Online: www. docsouth.unc.edu/leconte/leconte.html.

———. *Ware Sherman: A Journal of Three Months' Personal Experience in the Last Days of the Confederacy*. Berkeley: University of California Press, 1937.

Eliza Lord

Lord, William W., Jr. "A Child at the Siege of Vicksburg." *Harper's Monthly Magazine* 118 (December 1908–May 1909): 44–53.

Reed, Lida Lord. "A Woman's Experience during the Siege of Vicksburg." *The Century Illustrated Monthly Magazine* 61, no. 6 (April 1901).

Walker, Peter F. *Vicksburg: A People at War, 1860–1865*. Chapel Hill: University of North Carolina Press, 1960.

Ransom Powell

"Andersonville Civil War Prison—Historical Background." The National Park Services Web site. Online: www.cr.nps.gov/seac/histback.htm.

McElroy, John. *This Was Andersonville*. Edited by Roy Meredith. New York: McDowell, Obolensky Inc., 1957.

Powell, Ransom. *The Civil War Memoirs of Little Red Cap, A Drummer Boy at Andersonville Prison*. Edited by Harold L. Scott Sr. Cumberland, Md.: privately printed, 1997.

Opie Percival Read

"Alice Williamson Diary." Duke University Special Collections Library. Online: scriptorium.lib.duke.edu/williamson/.

Ash, Stephen V. "Sharks in an Angry Sea: Civilian Resistance and Guerrilla Warfare in Occupied Middle Tennessee, 1862–1865." *Tennessee Historical Quarterly* 45, no. 3 (Fall 1986): 217–29.

Baird, Reed A. "Opie Read: An American Traveler." *Tennessee Historical Quarterly* 32 (Spring–Winter 1974): 410–28.

Bergeron, Paul H. *Paths of the Past: Tennessee, 1770–1970*. Knoxville: University of Tennessee Press, 1979.

Crutchfield, James A. *Tennesseans at War: Volunteers and Patriots in Defense of Liberty*. Nashville: Rutledge Hill Press, 1987.

Durham, Walker T., ed. "Looking Every Minute for Them to Come." *Tennessee Historical Quarterly* 59, no. 2 (Summer 2000): 108–13.

Elfer, Maurice. *Opie Read*. Detroit, Mich.: Boyten Miller Press, 1940.

Morris, Robert L. *Opie Read, American Humorist*. New York: Helios Books, 1965.

Read, Opie. *I Remember*. New York: Richard R. Smith, Inc., 1930.

Ella Sheppard

Harding, Leonard. "The Cincinnati Riots of 1862." *Bulletin of the Cincinnati History Society* (October 1967): 229–39.

Howse, Beth. "Ella Sheppard (Moore), 1851–1914." Tennessee State University Web site. Online: www.tnstate.edu/library/digital/sheppard.htm.

Lovett, Bobby L. *The African-American History of Nashville, Tennessee 1780–1930*. Fayetteville: University of Arkansas Press, 1999.

Toppin, Edgar A. "Humbly They Served: The Black Brigade in the Defense of Cincinnati." *Journal of Negro History* 48, no. 2 (April 1963): 75–97.

Ward, Andrew. *Dark Midnight When I Rise: The Story of the Jubilee Singers*. New York: Farrar, Straus and Giroux, 2000.

Elisha Stockwell Jr.

Abernethy, Byron R., ed. *Private Elisha Stockwell, Jr. Sees the Civil War*. Norman: University of Oklahoma Press, 1958.

"Fourteenth Wisconsin Infantry Regiment." Wisconsin Veterans Museum. Online: badger.state.wi.us/agencies/dva/museum/cwregts/14wisinf.html.

Houghton, Edgar P. "History of Company I, Fourteenth Wisconsin Infantry from October 19, 1861, to October 9, 1865." *Wisconsin Magazine of History* 11, no. 1 (September 1927): 26–49.

John Sergeant Wise

Conrad, James Lee. *The Young Lions: Confederate Cadets at War*. Mechanicsburg, Pa.: Stackpole Books, 1997.

Wise, Barton H. *The Life of Henry A. Wise of Virginia*. New York: The Macmillan Company, 1899.

Wise, John S. *The End of an Era*. New York: Houghton, Mifflin and Company, 1899.

INDEX

African-American History of Nashville, Tennessee, The, 32

Agassiz, Louis, 123

Allegheny Arsenal, 11

Anderson, George Burgwyn, 149

Andersonville prison, 43–45

Antietam, Battle of, 148–49

Appomattox Court House, 10

Archer, Fletcher, 104–5, 106

Autry, James L., 95

Baird, Reed A., 84

Ball, Thomas, 33

Banister, Anne Augusta, 104–11

Banister, Blair, 108, 110

Banister, Mary Caroline, 106–7, 109, 110

Banister, Mollie, 106, 107

Banister, Norborne, 107, 108

Banister, William Constable, 104–5, 107

Banks, Nathaniel P., 70, 72, 73

Barton, Clara, 51

Beasley, Mary, 48

Beaufort, South Carolina, 53

Beauregard, P. G. T., 87, 106

Bell, John, 4

Belle Isle prison, 42

Berry, Jane, 27

Beverly, West Virginia, 38, 40

"Black Brigade, The," 36

Black River Falls, Wisconsin, 57

Blocker, Albert Butler, 132–41

Blocker, Albert Butler (son of Albert Butler Blocker), 141

Blocker, Charles Preston, 141

Blocker, Douglas Vaughn, 141

Blocker, Eliza Jane Webster, 141

Blocker, Eliza Miriam, 141

Blocker, Eugene, 134, 135, 139

Blocker, Eugenie Burrus, 141

Blocker, Frank, 134–35, 140

Blocker, Frank Harwood, 141

Blocker, Louis Edwin, 141

Blocker, Mary Douglass Butler, 134, 141

Blocker, Mary Steele, 141

Blocker, Westwood Wallace, 141

Blocker, William Johnston, 134

Blocker, William Preston, 134, 135, 137, 141

Blocker, William Webster, 141

Blouis, James, 48, 50

Bolling, Robert, 107

Booth, John Wilkes, 10

Boyd, Harry, 33

Branch, Lawrence O'Brien, 146

Breckinridge, John C., 4, 68, 119

Brown, John, 112, 114

Brown, Rev. John Mifflin, 66, 73

Buchanan, James, 85

Bull Run, Battle of, 87, 91–92

Burgwyn, Anna Greenough, 143–45

Burgwyn, Collinson Pierrepont Edwards, 143

Burgwyn, George Pollok, 143

Burgwyn, Henry King, 143–45

Burgwyn, Henry King, Jr., 143

Burgwyn, John, 143

Burgwyn, John Alveston, 143

Burgwyn, John Collinson, 143

Burgwyn, Margaret Carlisle Dunlop, 151

Burgwyn, Maria Greenough, 143

Burgwyn, William H. S., 142–51

Burlington, New Jersey, 7

Butler, Benjamin F., 68–69, 70

Cabell, Sergeant, 119

Calhoun, John C., 85

Campbell, Benjamin Bakewell, 14, 15

Campbell, Lois, 14, 15

Campbell, Maggie, 11–19

Campbell, Margaretta Wade, 13

Campbell, Nannie, 14

Campbell, Sample, 14

Camp Saxton, 52–53

Camp Sumpter, 43

Chattanooga, Tennessee, 7
Chelsea House, 107
Cincinnati, Ohio, 33–36
City Point, Virginia, 7–8
Clark, Henry T., 145
Clark, Walter, 148
Clingman, Thomas L., 150, 151
Clowning through Life, 22
Columbia, South Carolina, 128–29
Cooper, Douglas, 138
Corinth, Mississippi, 5, 63
Cozart, Colonel, 139–40
Crowder, Jacob, 65
Crowder, John Henry, 65–73
Crowder, Martha Ann Spencer, 65, 69,
    70, 71, 73
Cummings, James, 51
Cupid (pony), 99
Curly, 59, 61
Cutts, James Madison, Jr., 87

Dark Midnight When I Rise, 34
David Copperfield, 77
Davis, Edward, 51
Davis, Elizabeth Nisbet, 131
Davis, Henry Campbell, 131
Davis, Isabella Harper, 131
Davis, Jeff, Jr., 92
Davis, Jefferson, 12, 85, 91–92
Davis, Joe, 92
Davis, Joseph LeConte, 131
Davis, Maggie, 92
Davis, Mr., 127, 129, 130
Davis, Robert Means (husband of Sallie
    LeConte Davis), 130–31
Davis, Robert Means (son of Sallie
    LeConte Davis), 131
Davis, Sallie LeConte, 122–31
Davis, Sarah LeConte, 131
Day, W. A., 108, 111
Defoe, Daniel, 77
Deland, Emily, 19
Deland, Lorin, 19
Deland, Maggie Campbell, 11–19
Dickens, Charles, 77
Dimmock Line, 106, 108
Donnellan, Lieut., 101

Douglas, Addie Cutts, 85, 89
Douglas, Stephen A., 4, 85
Duvall, Lee, 93
Duvall, Rose Greenhow, 85–93
Duvall, William Penn, 93
Dwight, William, Jr., 72

Eckhart Mines, Maryland, 38
"Eddie Foy and the Seven Little Foys," 27
Elfer, Maurice, 77–78, 82, 83, 84
Ellis, John Willis, 105, 145
Emancipation Proclamation, 24–25
End of an Era, The, 114, 115, 116,
    118, 119
Enrollment and Conscription Act, 24–27

First South Carolina Volunteers, 51
Fitzgerald, Catherine, 22, 23
Fitzgerald, Edwin, 20–27
Fitzgerald, Ellen (mother of Edwin
    Fitzgerald), 22–24
Fitzgerald, Ellen (sister of Edwin
    Fitzgerald), 22, 24
Fitzgerald, Lizzie, 88, 89
Fitzgerald, Mary, 22
Fitzgerald, Richard, 22–24
Fond du Lac, Wisconsin, 57, 59–60
Fort Donelson, 78
Forten, Charlotte L., 52
Fort Gregg, 54
Fort Henry, 78
Fort Pulaski, 47–50
Foy, Eddie, 20–27
François, Sergeant, 70
Franklin, Benjamin, 83
Fredericksburg, Battle of, 149
Frostburg Mining Journal, 46
Furman, Emma Florence LeConte, 123,
    125, 128, 129–30
Furman, Farish Carter, 131

Galena, Illinois, 3, 5
Gallatin, Tennessee, 74–84
Gamble, Hamilton R., 135
Gervais, Adelaide, 56, 57
Gervais, Nicholas, 57
Gettysburg, Battle of, 16

Gibson, Charles W., 68
"Girl I Left Behind Me, The," 14
Gosport Navy Yard, 116–17
Graham, Billy, 14, 17
Grant, Chapman, 10
Grant, Elizabeth Chapman, 10
Grant, Fred, 3, 4, 6, 7
Grant, Jesse Root, 1–10
Grant, Julia Dent, 1–10
Grant, Lillian Burns Wilkins, 10
Grant, Nellie (daughter of Jesse Root
    Grant), 10
Grant, Nellie (sister of Jesse Root
    Grant), 3, 5
Grant, Orvil, 3
Grant, Simpson, 3
Grant, Ulysses S., 1–10, 60–61, 96,
    101, 102
Grant, Ulysses S., Jr., 3
Greenhow, Gertrude, 86
Greenhow, Leila, 86, 87
Greenhow, Robert, 85, 86
Greenhow, Rose, 85–93
Greenhow, Rose O'Neal, 85–93
Greenough, David Stoddard, 143
Greer, Elkanah Brackin, 135, 136–37

Hale, S. M., 136
Harden, Ada, 127, 128
Harden, Annie, 127
Harden, Jane, 122, 127, 128
Harpers Ferry, Virginia, 112, 114
Harris, Joel Chandler, 77, 83
Harris, Mr., 126
Higginson, Thomas Wentworth, 52–53
Hillside, 143, 145
Histories of the Several Regiments and
    Battalions from North Carolina in the
    Great War 1861–65, 146–47, 148
Holly Springs, Mississippi, 1
Houghton, David, 57, 62
Houghton, Edgar, 56–57, 61, 62
Howe, Henry, 36

If This Be I, As I Suppose It Be, 12, 18, 19
I Remember, 74, 76, 77, 79, 81–82

Jackson, Claiborne Fox, 135–36
Jarboe, James A., 41
Jeff (horse), 8–9
Johnson, R.W., 79, 82
Johnston, Albert S., 60
Johnston, Joseph E., 101, 150
Jones, George B., 107
Jones, Lewis, 44, 46
Joshua, 125–26
Jubilee Singers, 37

Kautz's Raiders, 106
Key to Uncle Tom's Cabin, The, 33
King, Edward, 51, 54–55
King, Susie Baker, 47–55

Lane, Walter Paye, 135, 138
LeConte, Caroline Eaton, 123, 130
LeConte, Caroline Nisbet, 123, 129
LeConte, Joseph, 122–31
LeConte, Josephine Eloise, 123
LeConte, Sallie, 122–31
Lee, Mary Tabb Bolling, 111
Lee, Robert E., 10, 108–9, 111, 120
Lee, Rooney, 111
Lewis, Captain, 71
Lilah, 76–77
Lincoln, Abraham, 4–5, 8–10, 27, 34,
    38, 66–67, 76
Lincoln, Tad, 8–10
Lord, Eliza, 94–103
Lord, Louisa, 94, 97, 100, 103
Lord, Margaret Stockton, 94–103
Lord, Sarah, 94, 97, 103
Lord, William W., 94–103
Lord, Willie, 94, 97, 98, 99, 100, 102–3
Lovett, Bobby L., 32
Lyon, Nathaniel, 136–37

Mammy Viney, 29
Maple Grove, 13
Marsh, Mrs., 71
McCulloch, Ben, 135–36
McDowell, Irvin, 87
McElroy, John, 43, 44, 46
Merriam, Mr., 98
Merrimack, 118

Monitor, 118
Moore, Clinton Fisk Russell, 37
Moore, Ella Sheppard, 28–37
Moore, Florence Greenhow, 86, 87,
    92, 93
Moore, George Sheppard, 37
Moore, George W., 37
Moore, Sarah Elizabeth, 37
Moore, Thomas D., 67
Moore, Treadwell, 87, 93
Morgan, John Hunt, 16–17, 79, 81–82
Morgan's Raiders, 17, 79, 81–82
Morris, Robert L., 83
Moses, Mark E., 45
My Imprisonment, 88
My Young Masters, 83

Napoleon III (emperor of France), 92
Nashville, Tennessee, 28–32
Native Guards, 67–73
New Bern, Battle of, 146
New Creek, West Virginia, 40
New Market, Battle of, 119
New Mr. Howerson, The, 83
New Orleans, Battle of, 66
New Orleans, Louisiana, 65–71
New York, New York, 20–27

O'Connor, Katie, 48
Odd Folks, 83
Old Capitol Prison, 85–86, 89–91
Opothleyahola, 138–39

Paine, Eleazar Arthur, 82–83
Parsons, Walter, 45
Pemberton, John C., 101, 102
Petersburg, Virginia, 8, 10, 104–11
Pettigrew, James Johnston, 147
Phillips, Wendell, 35
Pinkerton, Allan, 87–88
Pittsburgh, Pennsylvania, 11
Pittsburg Landing, Tennessee, 60–61
Port Hudson, Louisiana, 71–73
Powell, Escha May, 46
Powell, James (father of Ransom
    Powell), 38–40
Powell, James (son of Ransom Powell), 46

Powell, John, 46
Powell, Maggie Watson, 46
Powell, Mary, 38–40
Powell, Ransom, 38–46
Powell, Ransom, Jr., 46
Powell, William, 46
Pressley, J., 33
Preston, Robert, 119–20
Price, Sterling, 135–36, 137
Pryor, Anne Augusta Banister, 104–11
Pryor, Archibald Campbell, 111

Ransom, Matt W., 146–47
Ransom, Robert, Jr., 147–48, 149
Ransom's Brigade, 147–48
Read, Ada Benham, 83
Read, Cordelia, 74
Read, Elaine, 83
Read, Elizabeth Wallace, 74, 76–77, 82
Read, Guilford, Jr., 74
Read, Guilford (father of Opie Percival
    Read), 74, 76–77, 82, 83
Read, Guilford (son of Opie Percival
    Read), 83
Read, Harriet (daughter of Opie Percival
    Read), 83
Read, Harriet (sister of Opie Percival
    Read), 74
Read, James, 74
Read, Leslie, 83
Read, Martha, 74
Read, Opie Percival, 74–84
Read, Philo, 83
Read, William, 74
Rebbie (pony), 6, 8–9
Red Cap, 38–46
Reed, Colin, 103
Reed, Colin McFarquhar, 103
Reed, Dolly, 48, 50
Reed, Eliza Lord, 94–103
Reed, Eva, 103
Reed, Lida, 103
Reed, Richard, 103
Reed, Robert, 103
Reed, William, 103
Richmond, Virginia, 91–92
"Robert the Good Shooter," 77

Robinson Crusoe, 77
Rolleston, 116
Rose, Victor M., 135, 136, 137–38, 139
Rosser, Thomas L., 41

Saltville, Battle of, 119–20
Savannah, Georgia, 47–50
Savannah, Georgia prison, 45
Saxton, Rufus, 51
Saylor's Creek, 120
Seabrooke, South Carolina, 53
Sea Islands, 50
Seddon, James A., 101
Semple, G. W., 42
Sergeant, John, 115
Shaw, Mary, 53–54
Sheppard, Cornelia, 29–34, 37
Sheppard, Ella, 28–37
Sheppard, Sarah, 28–29, 32, 36
Sheppard, Simon, 28–34, 36
Sigel, Franz, 119, 136
Sinclair, James, 146
Smith, Amanda Wright, 15–16
Smith, Don, 15–16
Smith, Kirby, 35
St. Simon's Island, 50–51
Stanton, Edwin M., 69
Stars, Thomas, 66, 73
Staubly, Godfrey, 107
Stiles, Mr., 96–98
Stockwell, Catherine Agnes Hurley, 64
Stockwell, Elisha, Jr., 56–64
Stockwell, Frank, 56
Stowe, Harriet Beecher, 33, 115–16
Sumner, William Hyslop, 143

Taylor, Russell L., 55
Taylor, Susie Baker King, 47–55
Texas Hunters, 134–35
Thirty-third United States Colored
    Troops, 54
This Was Andersonville, 43
Thompson, William H., 27
Thornbury, 145
Twain, Mark, 83

Uncle Tom's Cabin, 33, 115–16

Van Dorn, Earl, 1
Vicksburg, Mississippi, 5–6, 63, 94–103
Virginia, 118
Virginia Military Institute (VMI),
    118–19

Wadkins, Daniel, 31, 32
Wallace, George, 77, 82
Wallace, Lew, 35
Walter, Harvey W., 1
Walter Place, 1
Walthourville, Georgia, 126–27
Ward, Andrew, 34
Washington, Lewis, 114
Webster, John Brown, 141
Webster, Julia Maria Mead Steel, 141
Williams, Laura, 78
Williamson, Alice, 82–83
Wilson, Maria, 69
Wilson's Creek, Battle of, 136–37
Winder, John H., 43–44
Wirz, Henry, 44–45
Wise, Anne Jennings, 115
Wise, Ann Jennings, 115
Wise, Byrd Douglas, 121
Wise, Eva Douglas, 121
Wise, Evelyn Beverly Douglas, 121
Wise, Henry Alexander, Jr., 115, 117
Wise, Henry Alexander (father of John
    Sergeant Wise), 112–21
Wise, Henry Alexander (son of John
    Sergeant Wise), 121
Wise, Hugh Douglas, 121
Wise, Jennings Cropper, 121
Wise, John Sergeant, 112–21
Wise, John Sergeant, Jr., 121
Wise, Margaretta, 121
Wise, Margaretta Ellen, 115
Wise, Mary Elizabeth, 115
Wise, Mary Elizabeth Lyons, 115
Wise, Obadiah Jennings, 115, 117–18
Wise, Richard Alsop, 115, 117, 118
Wise, Sarah Sergeant, 115
Wood, William, 89
Woodhouse, Mary, 48

ABOUT THE AUTHOR

Scotti McAuliff Cohn's interest in the Civil War is personal. For one thing her great-great-grandfather, William Calvin Smith, served in the Confederate army. His experiences are preserved in his memoir, *The Private in Gray*. Family members still talk about Smith's displeasure at the marriage of his granddaughter (Scotti's grandmother) to a Yankee from New York.

Scotti was born and raised in Springfield, Illinois, where Abraham Lincoln, chief of all the Yankees, once lived and is now buried. By age ten she had lost track of the number of times she had visited the Great Emancipator's home and tomb.

After living for more than twenty years in North Carolina, Scotti moved back to the Land of Lincoln just in time to celebrate the new millennium. A freelance writer and editor specializing in health care, history, and young-adult fiction, her interests include music, travel, cats, and astrology.

Scotti has written two other books for The Globe Pequot Press, *More than Petticoats: Remarkable North Carolina Women* and *It Happened in North Carolina*.